DON CASTILLO'S MOST SEXIEST Women Art!

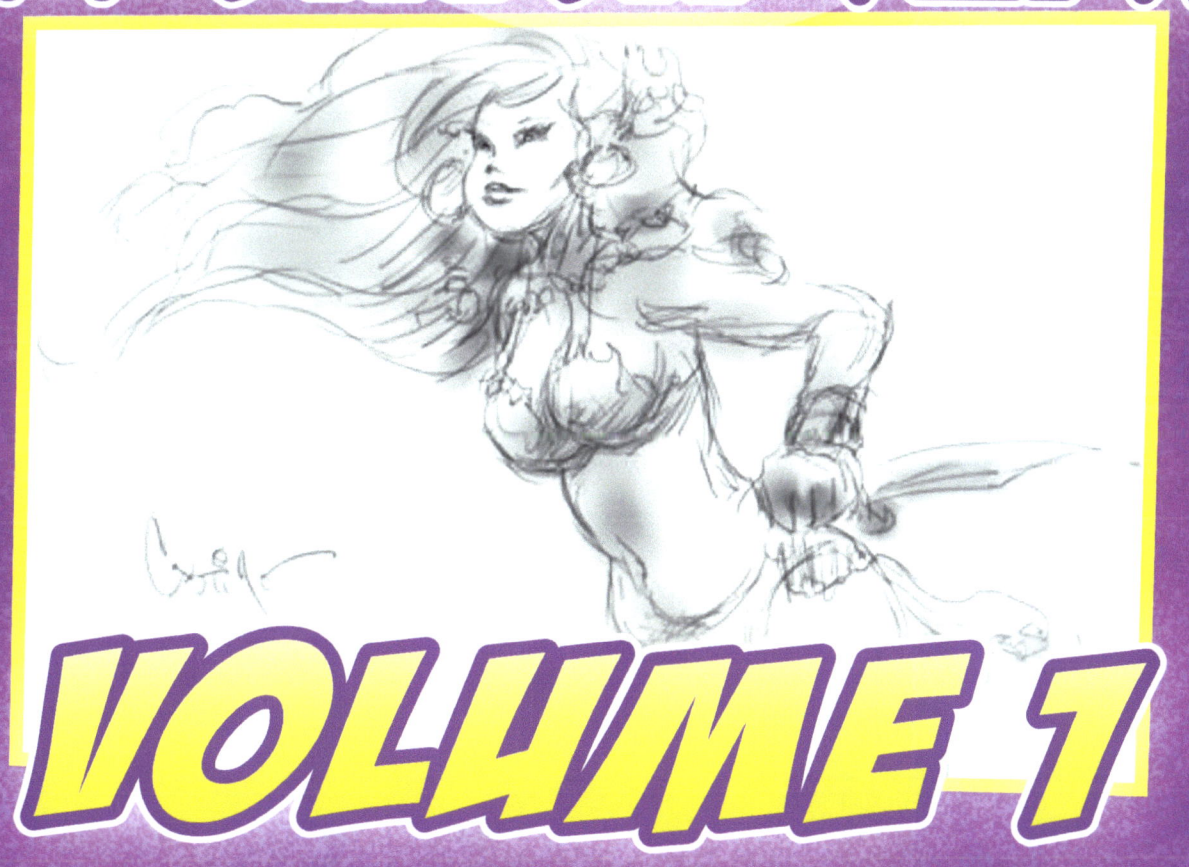

VOLUME 1

The Martial ARTist

Don Castillo, a San Antonio native, turns his love of karate into art through digital drawing.

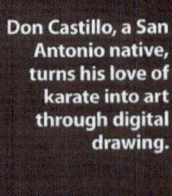

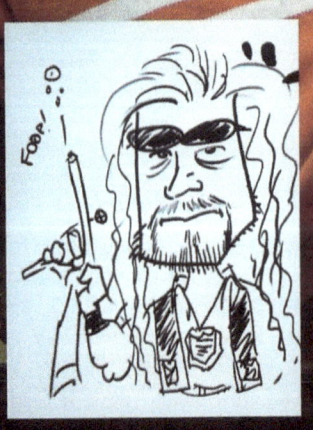
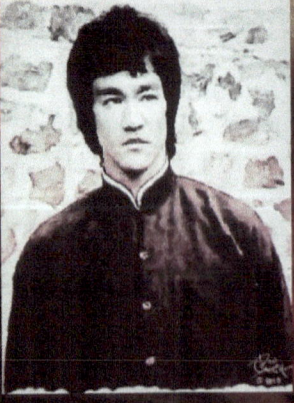
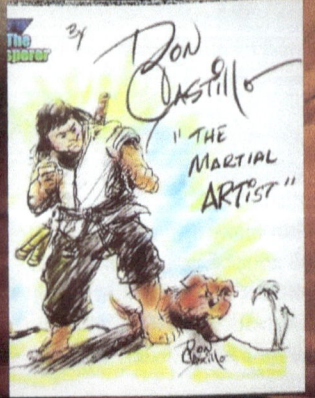
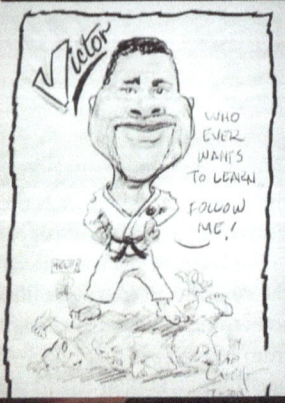

DEDICATION:

THANKS TO EVERYONE FOR BUYING THIS BOOK
AND ALL THE LOVE AND SUPPORT I GET FROM
MY FAMILY AND FRIENDS.
WRITE ME AT DONLEEJKD@AOL.COM OR FIND
ME AT DON CASTILLO ON FACEBOOK.COM

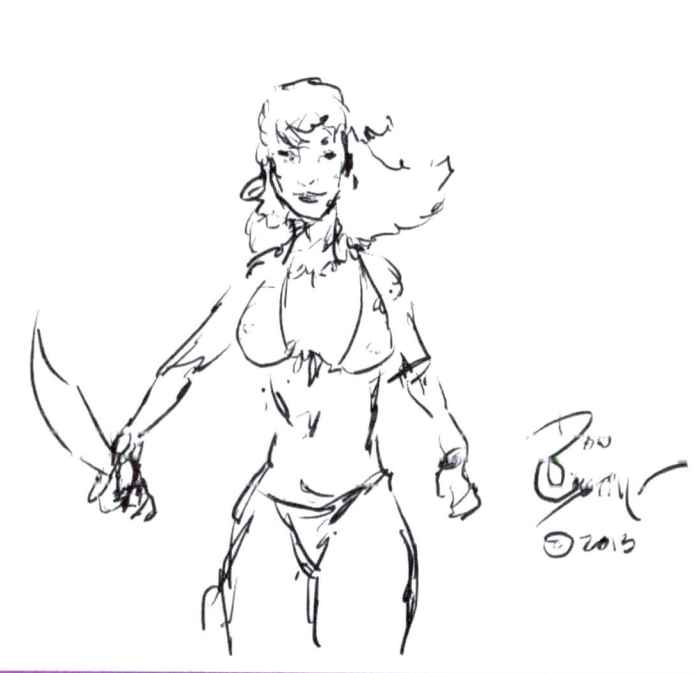

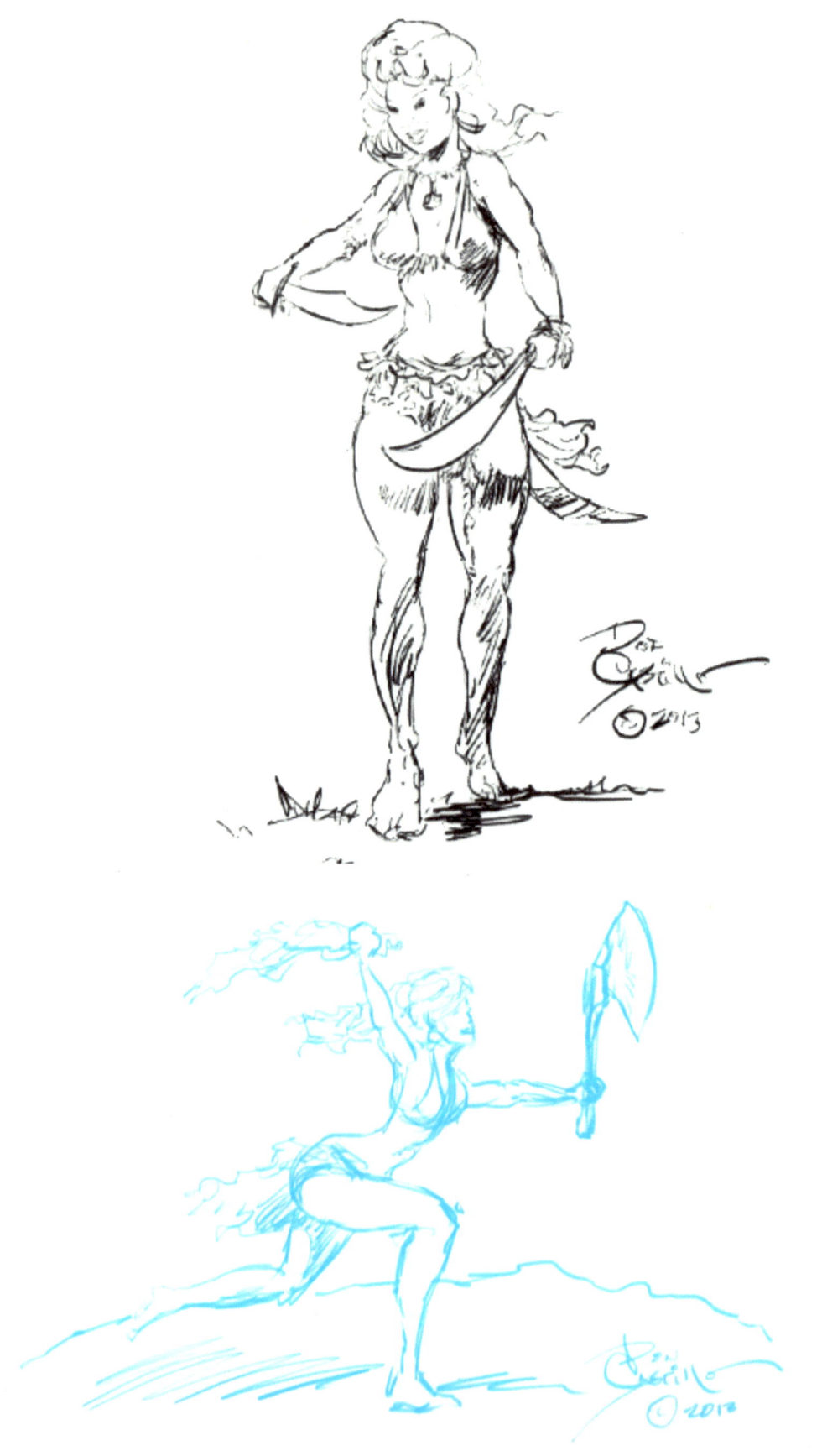

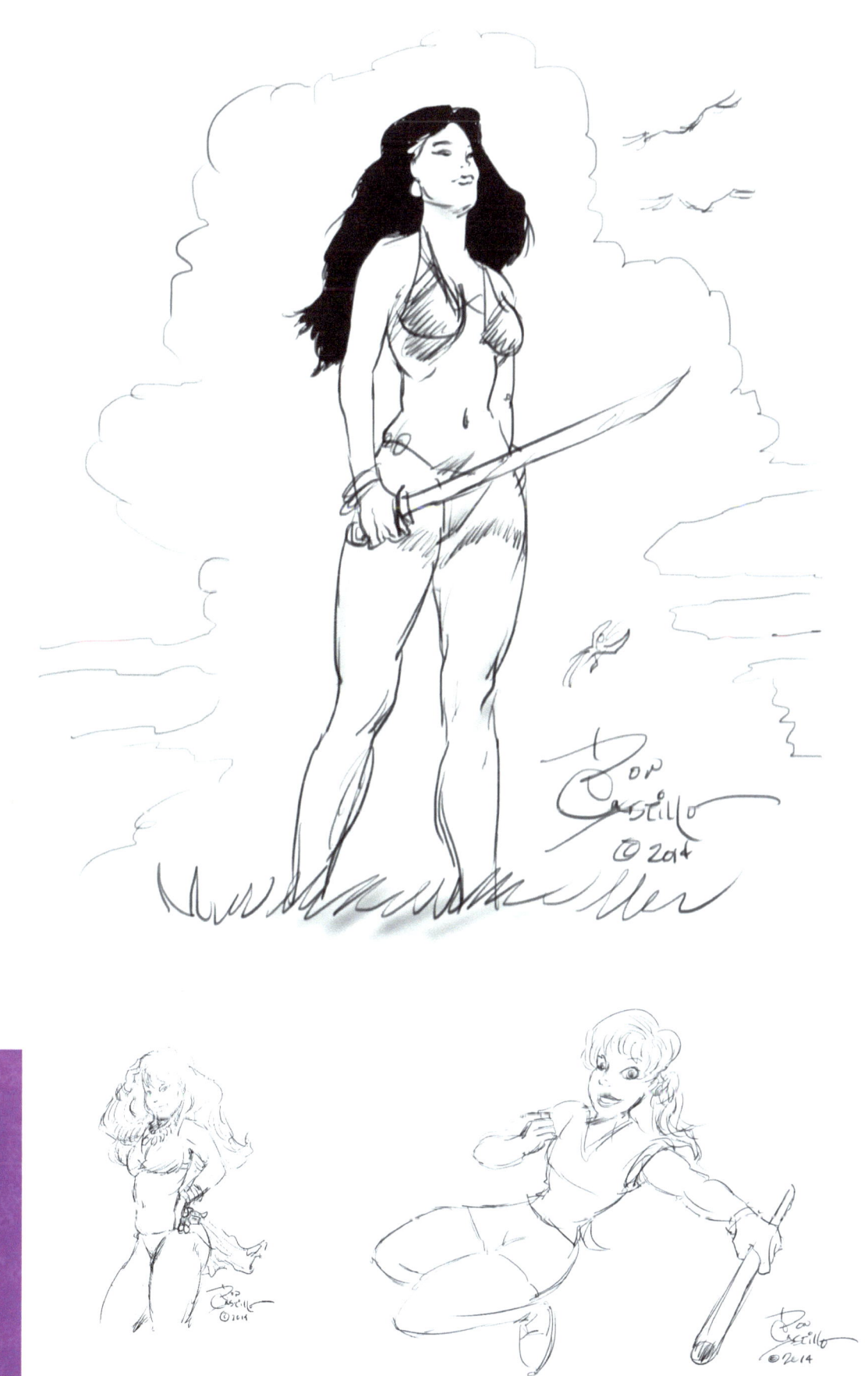

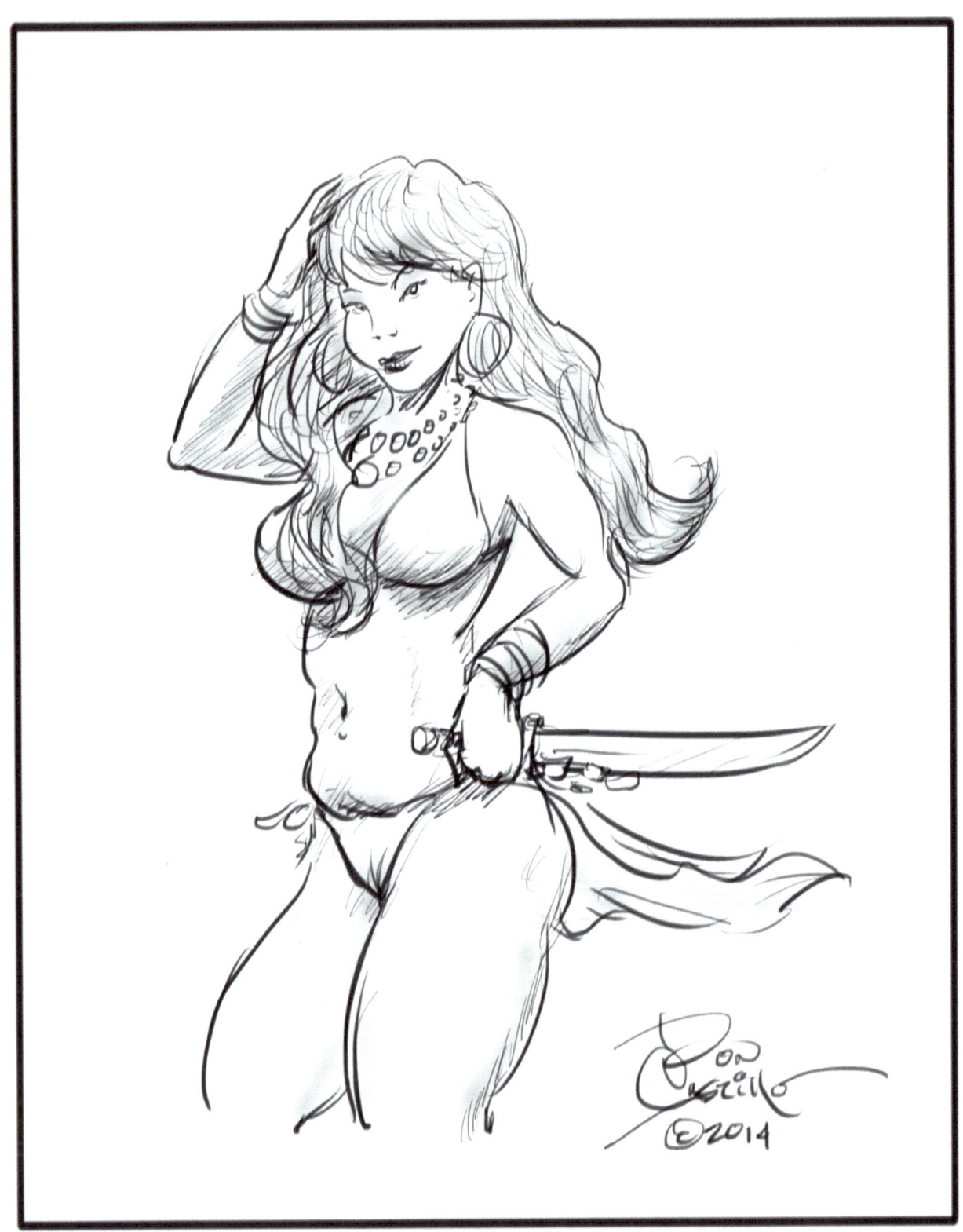

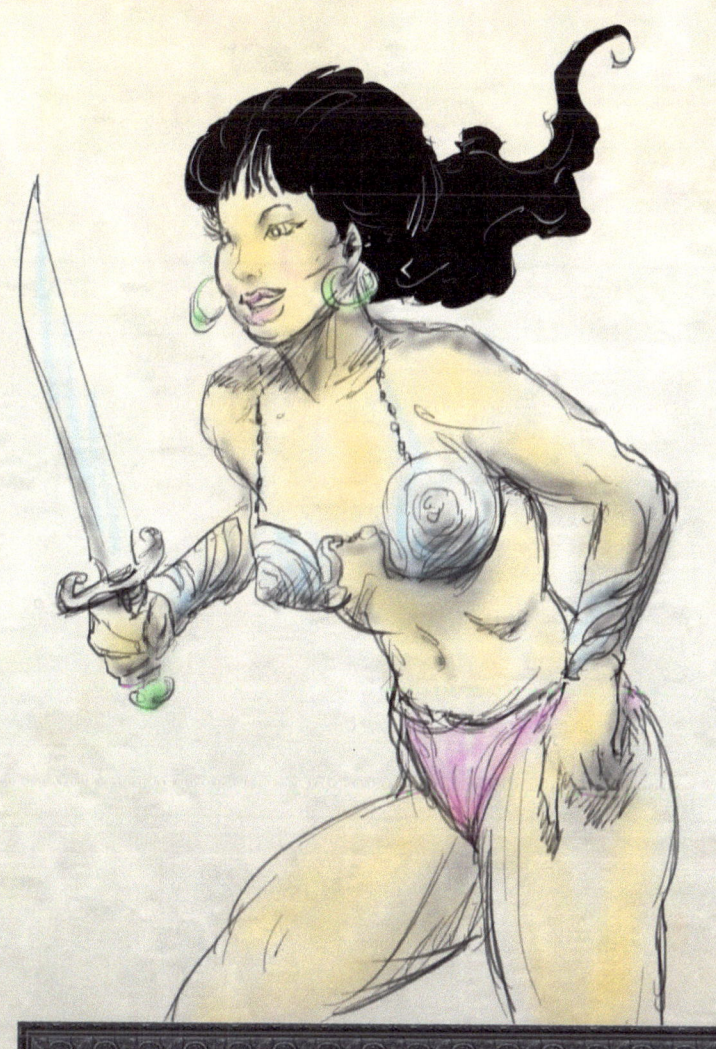
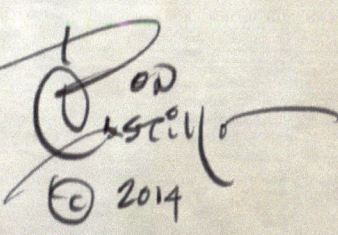
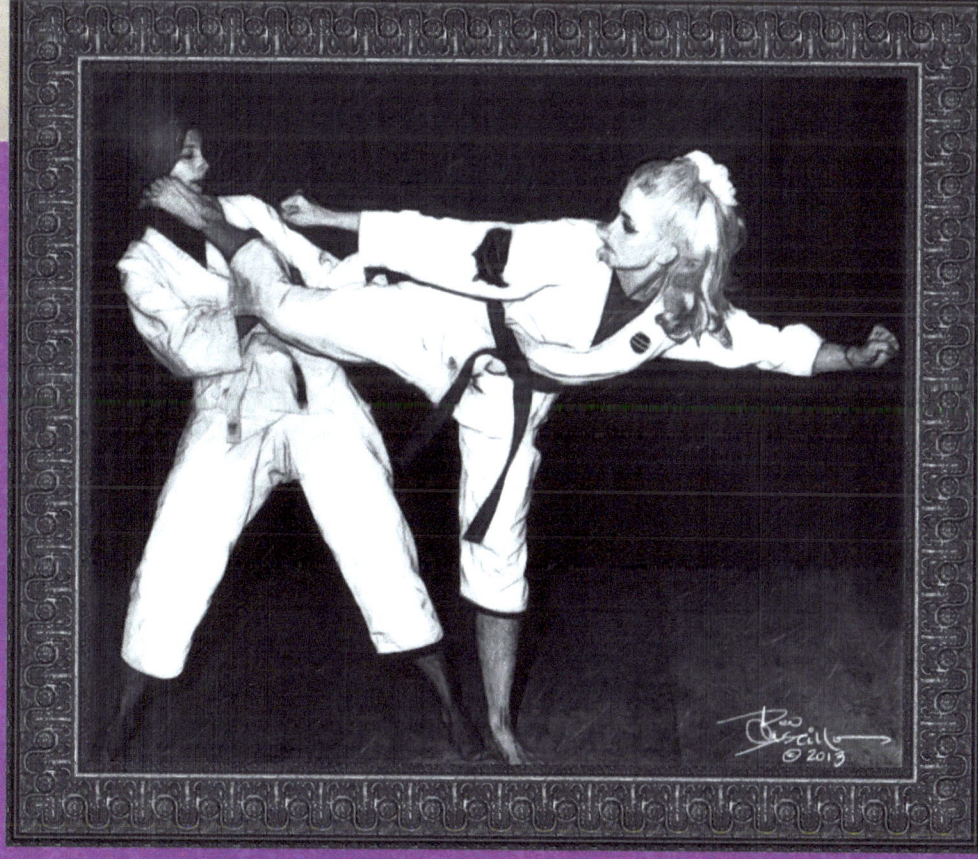

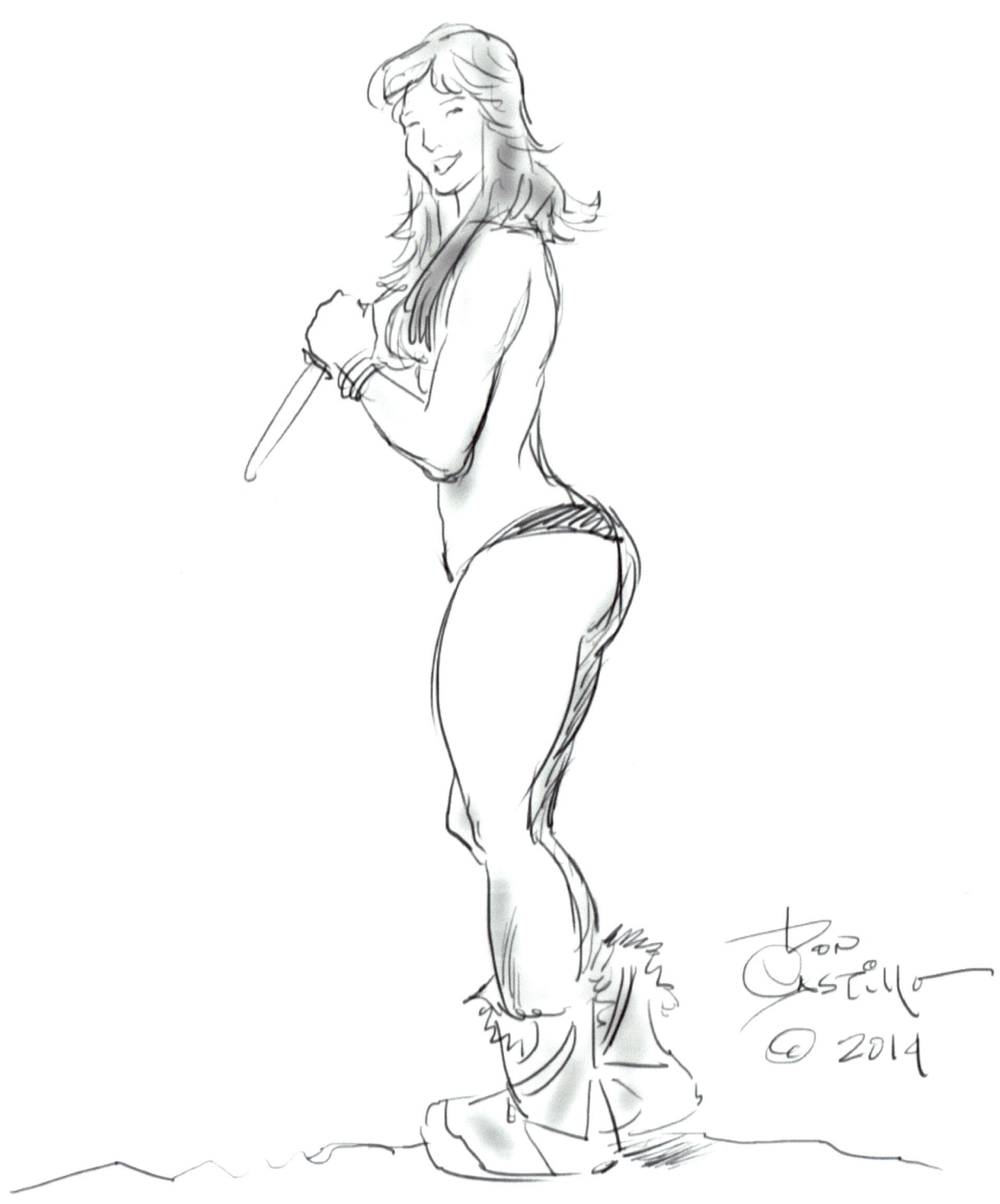

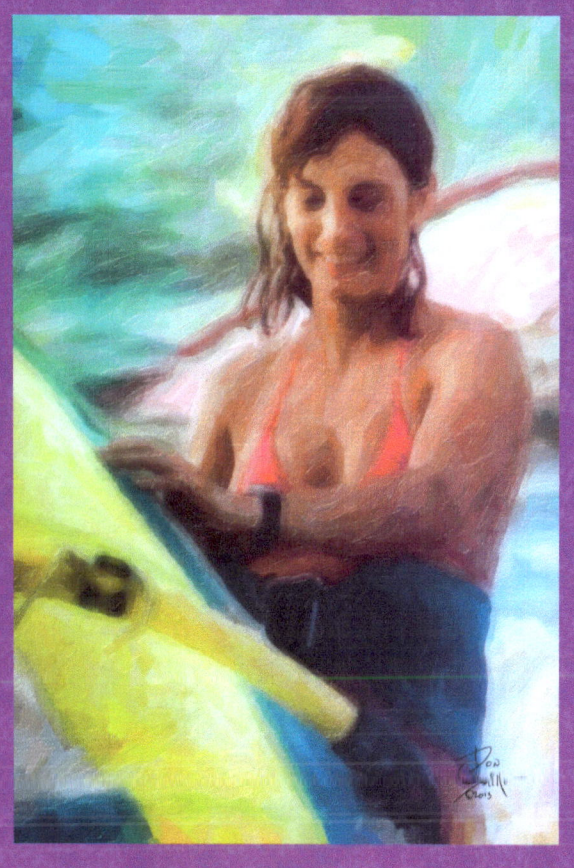

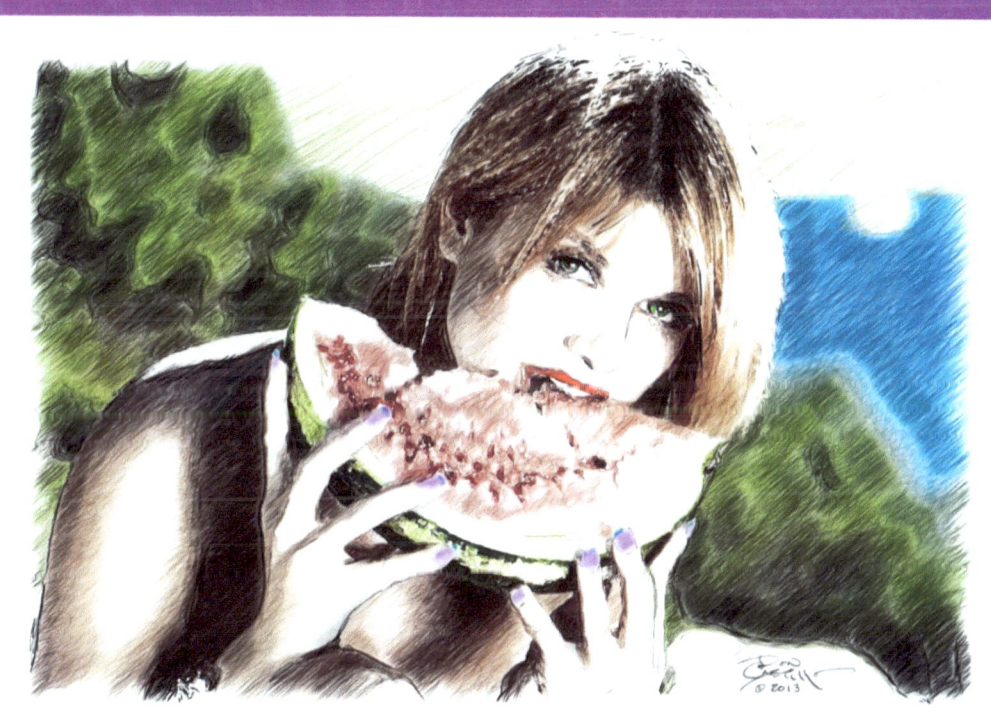

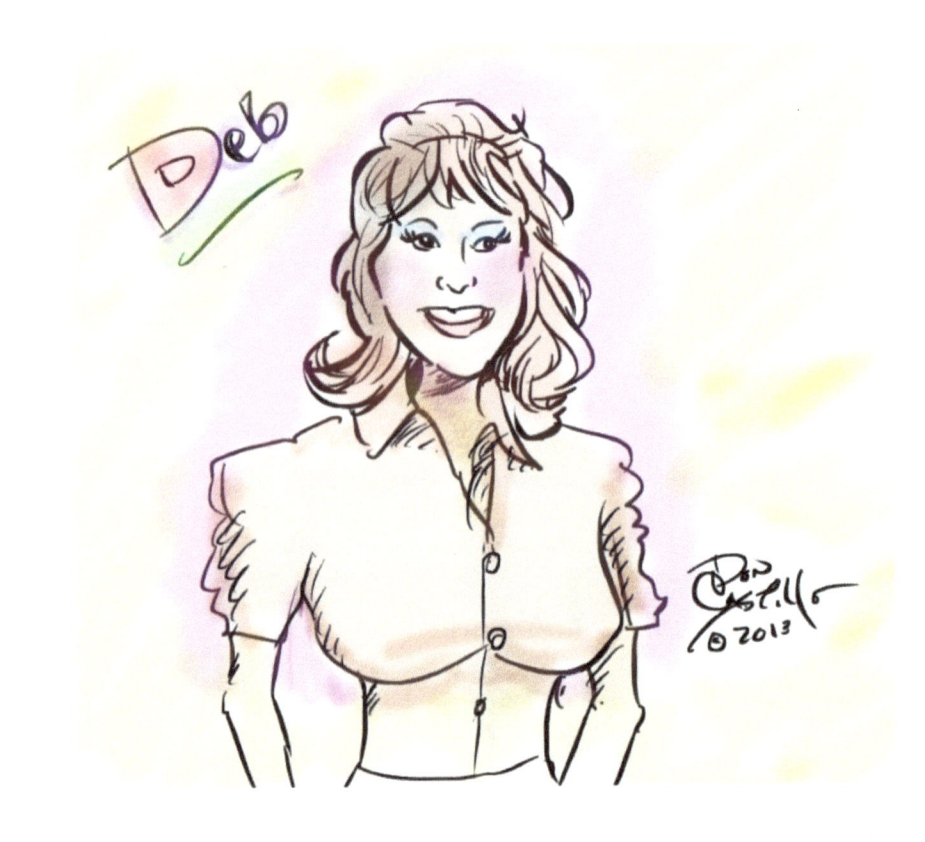

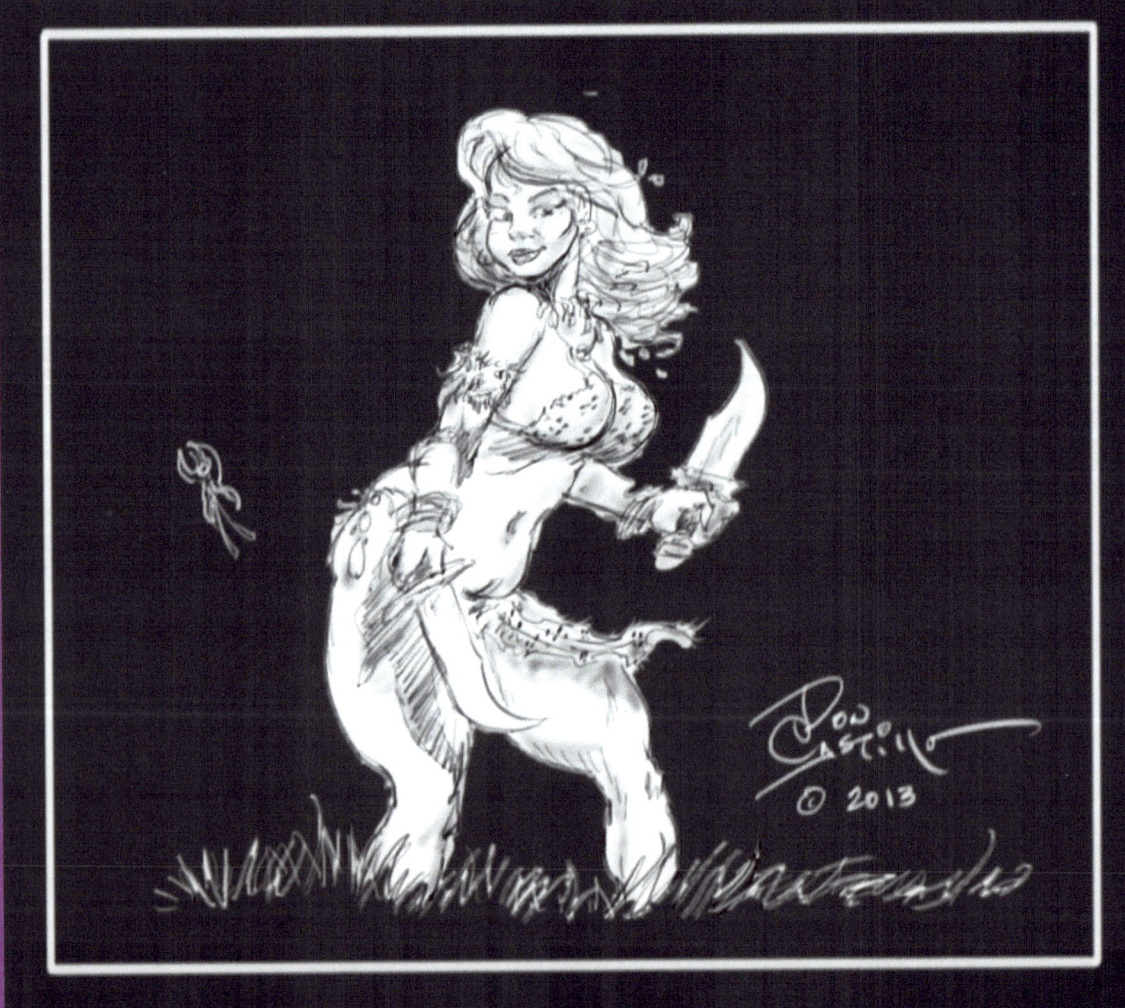

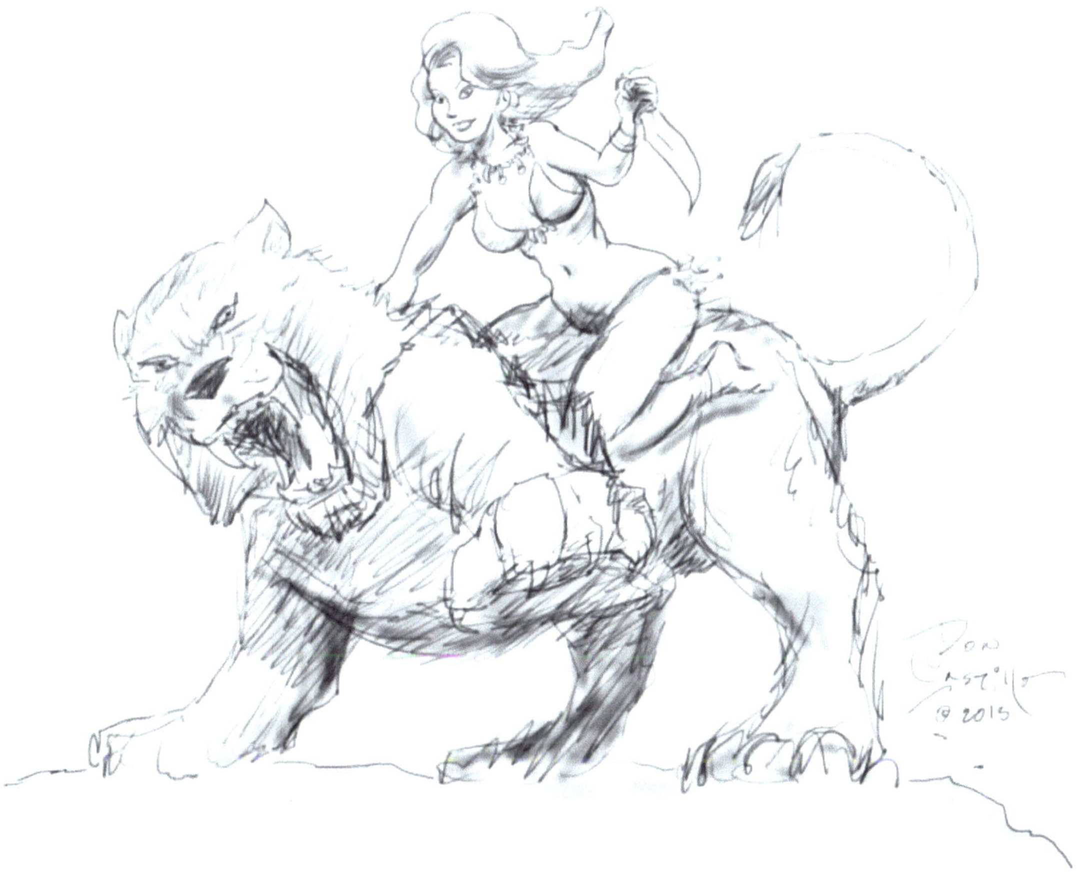

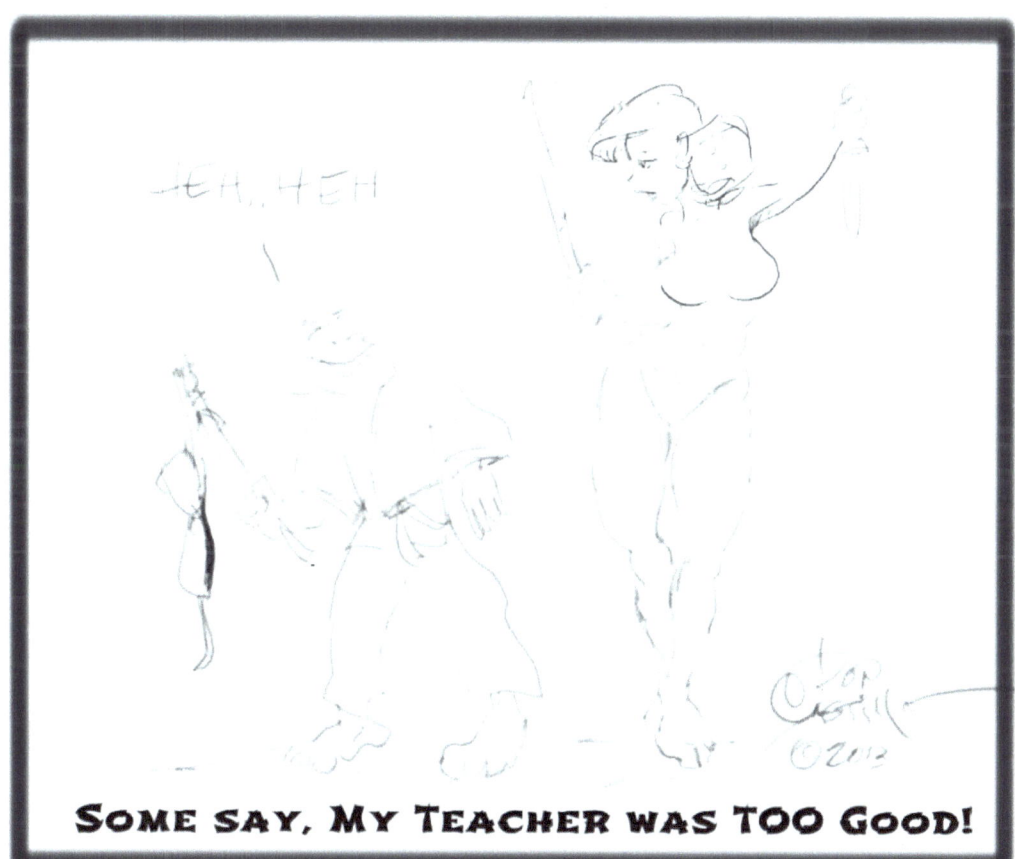

SOME SAY, MY TEACHER WAS TOO GOOD!

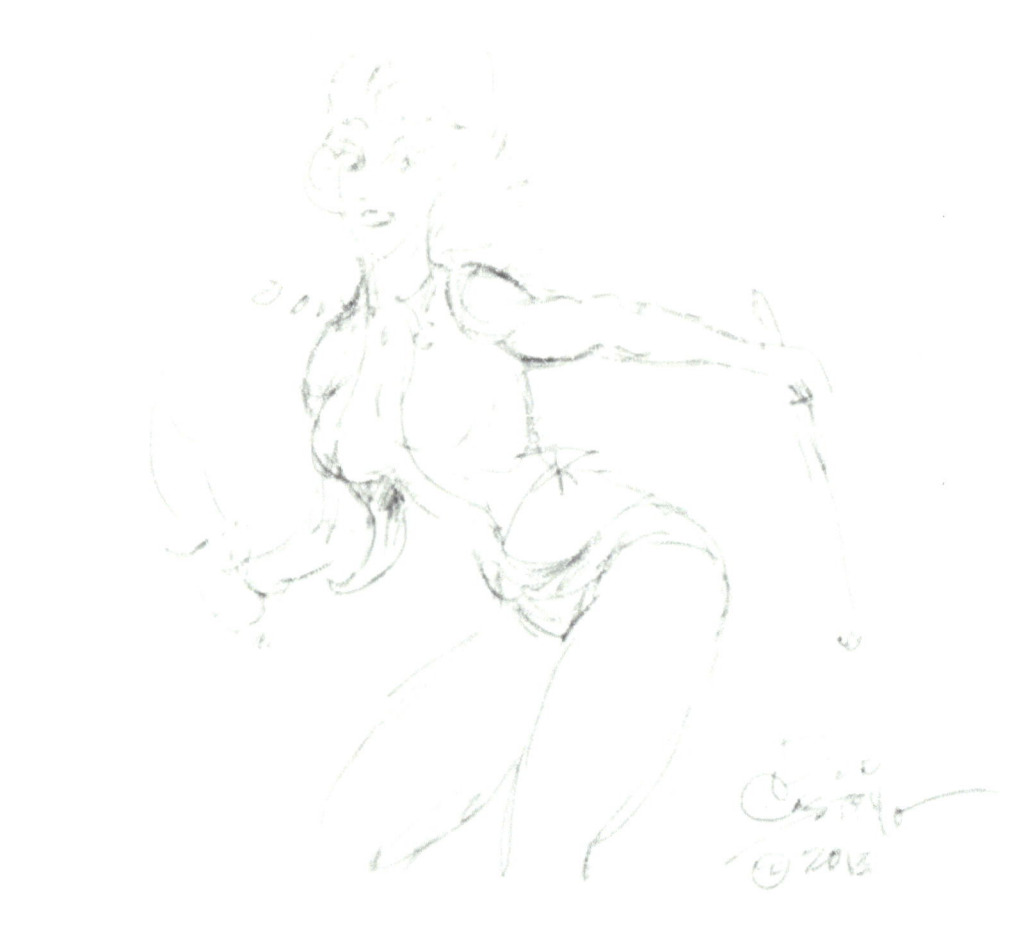

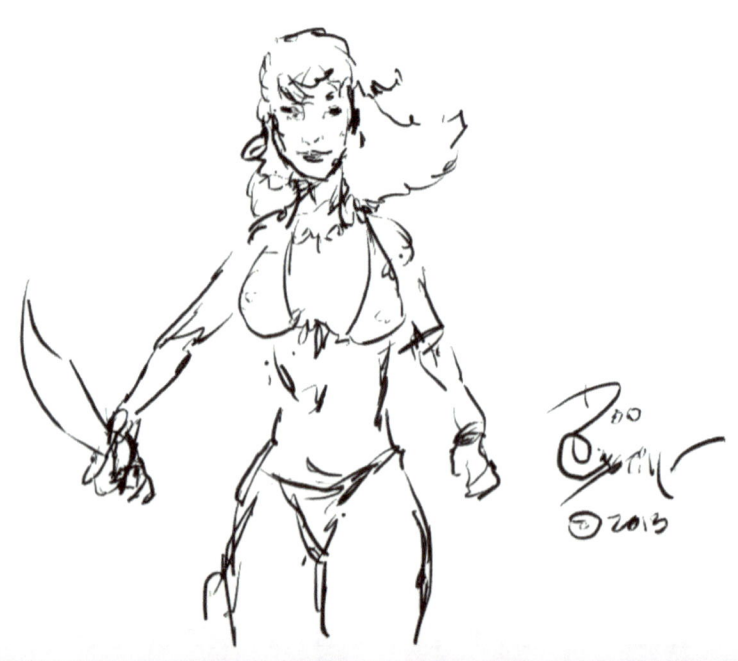

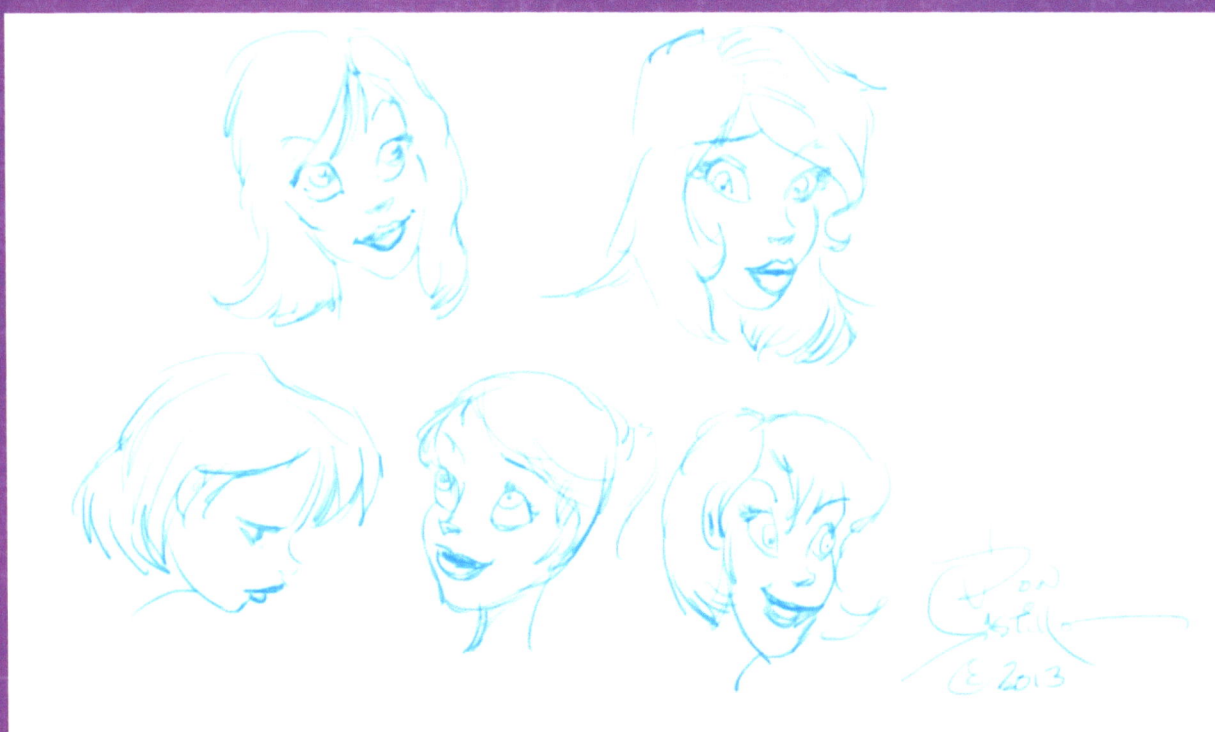

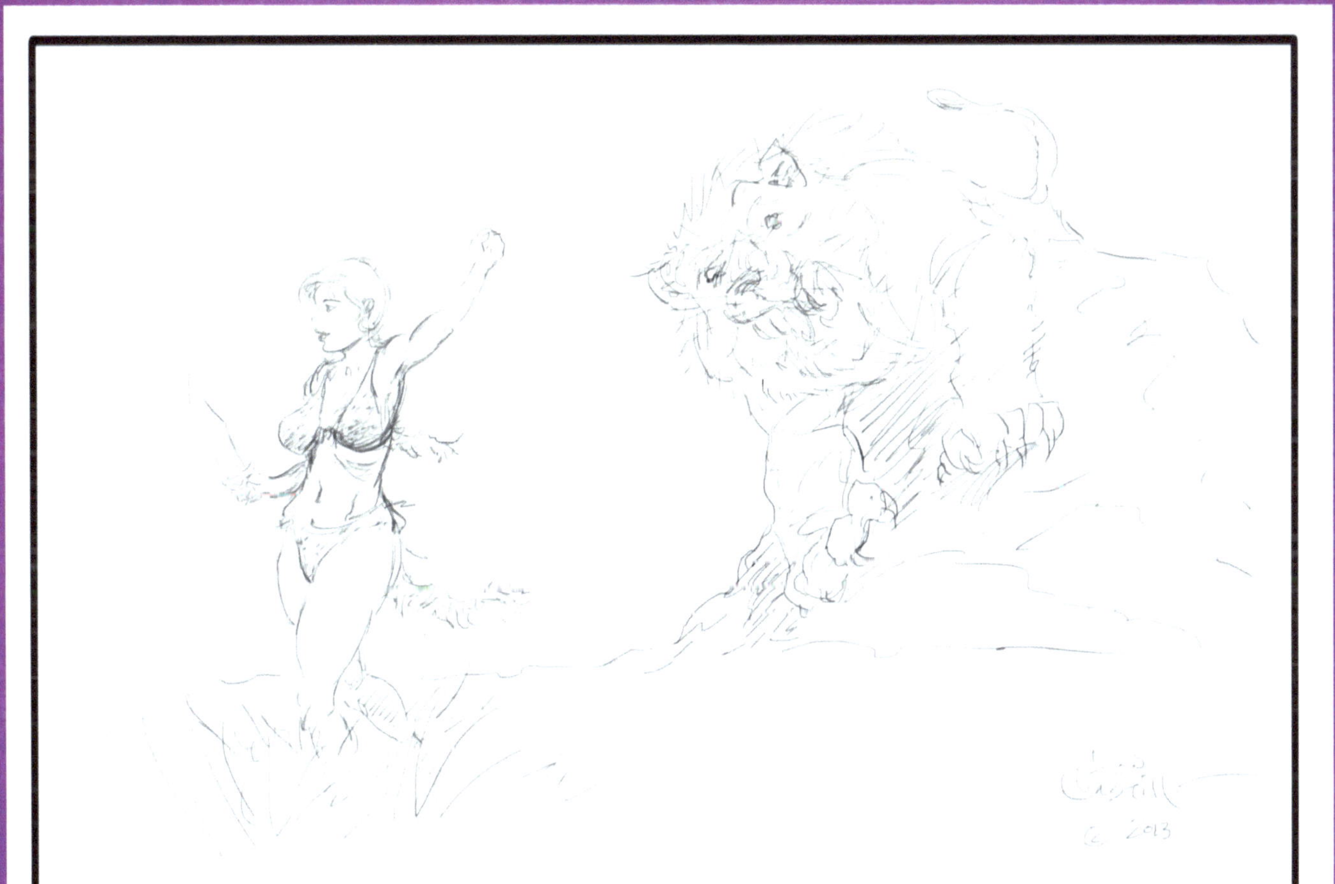

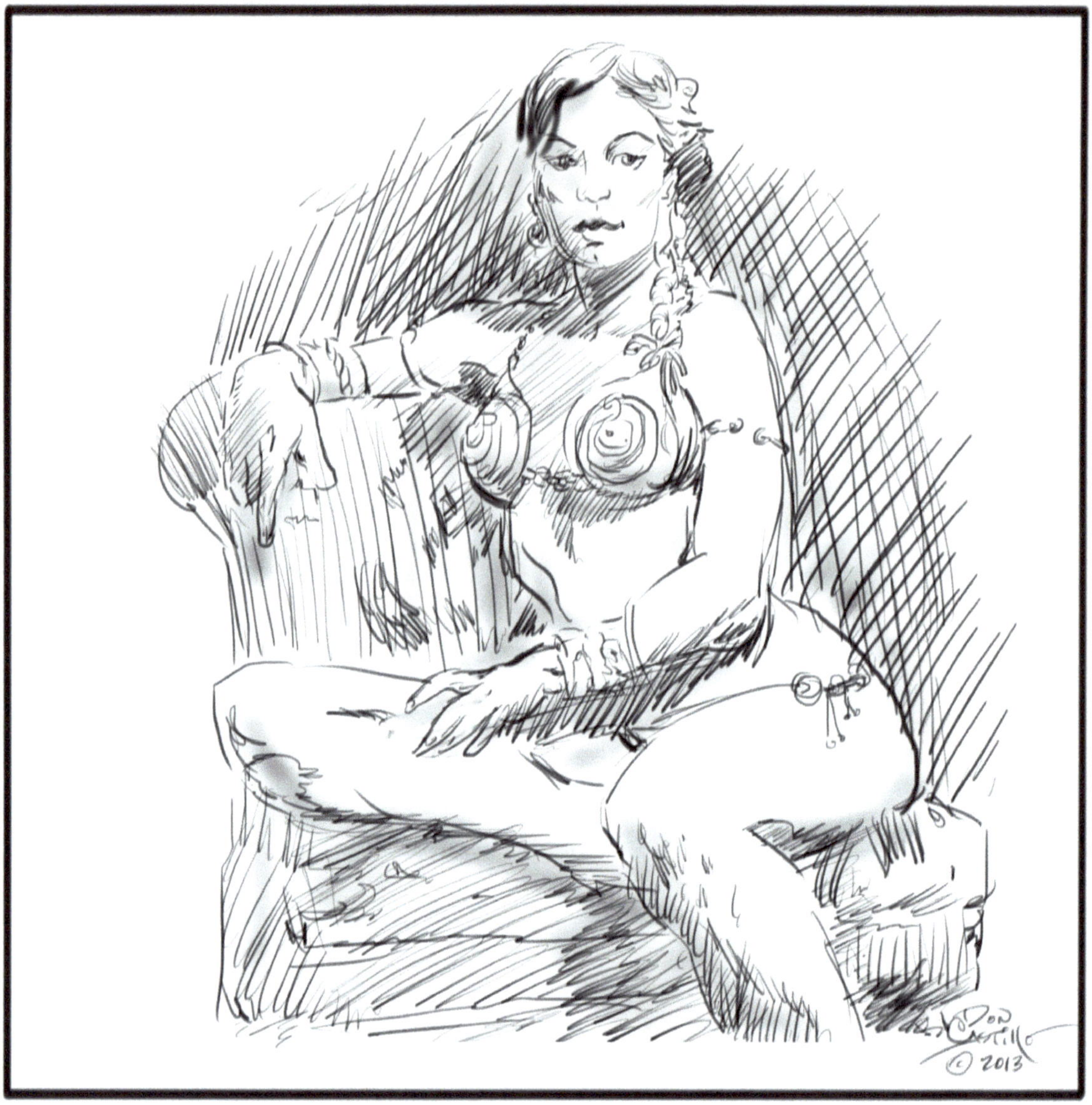

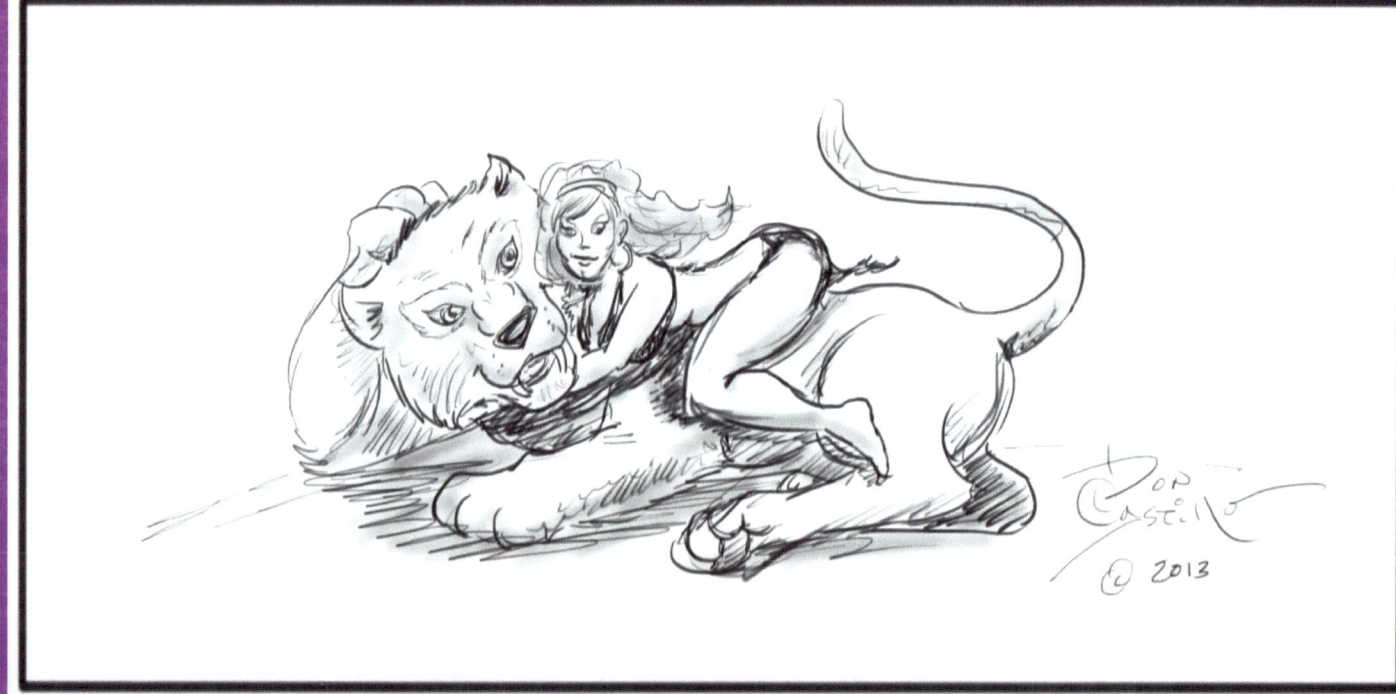

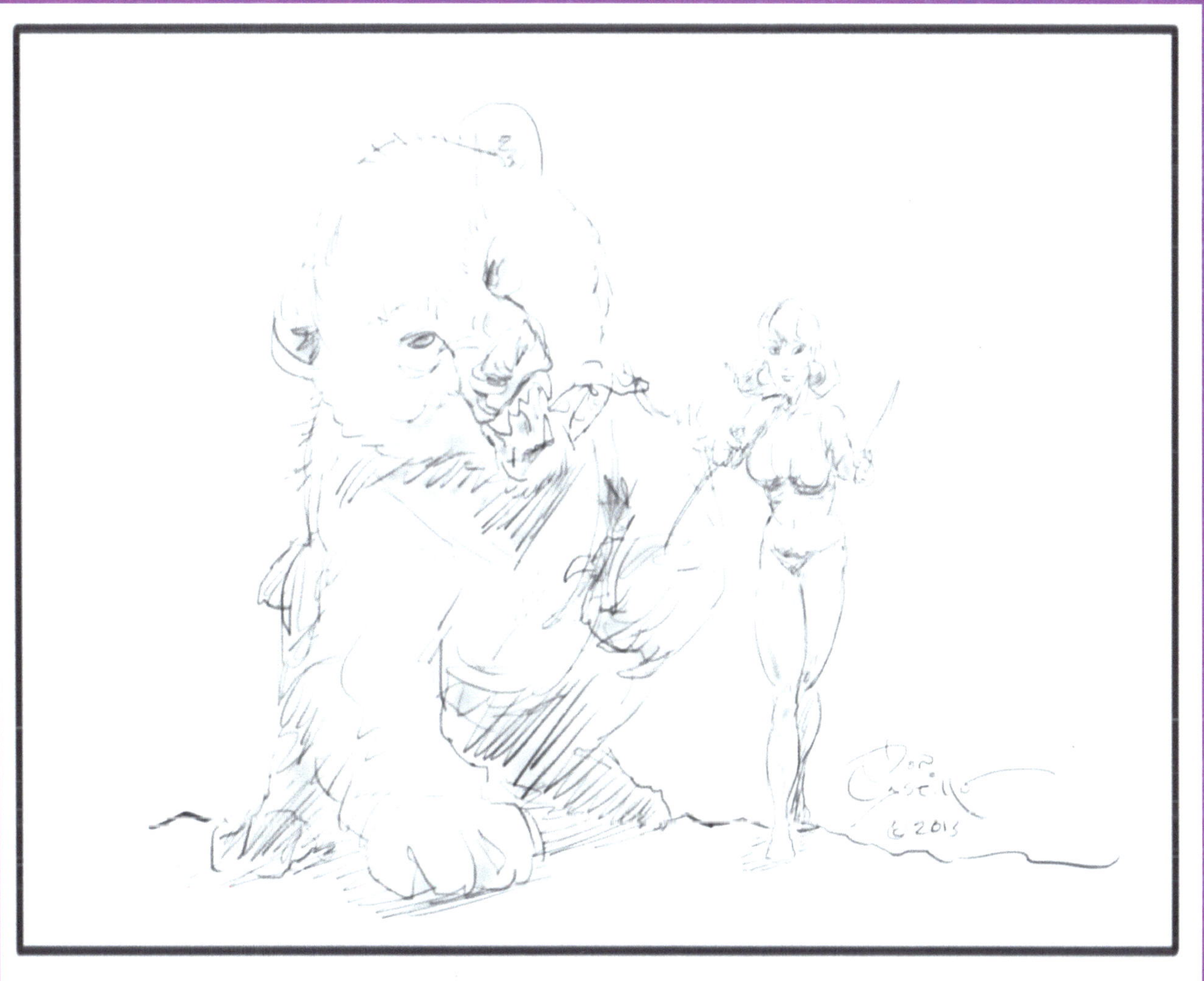

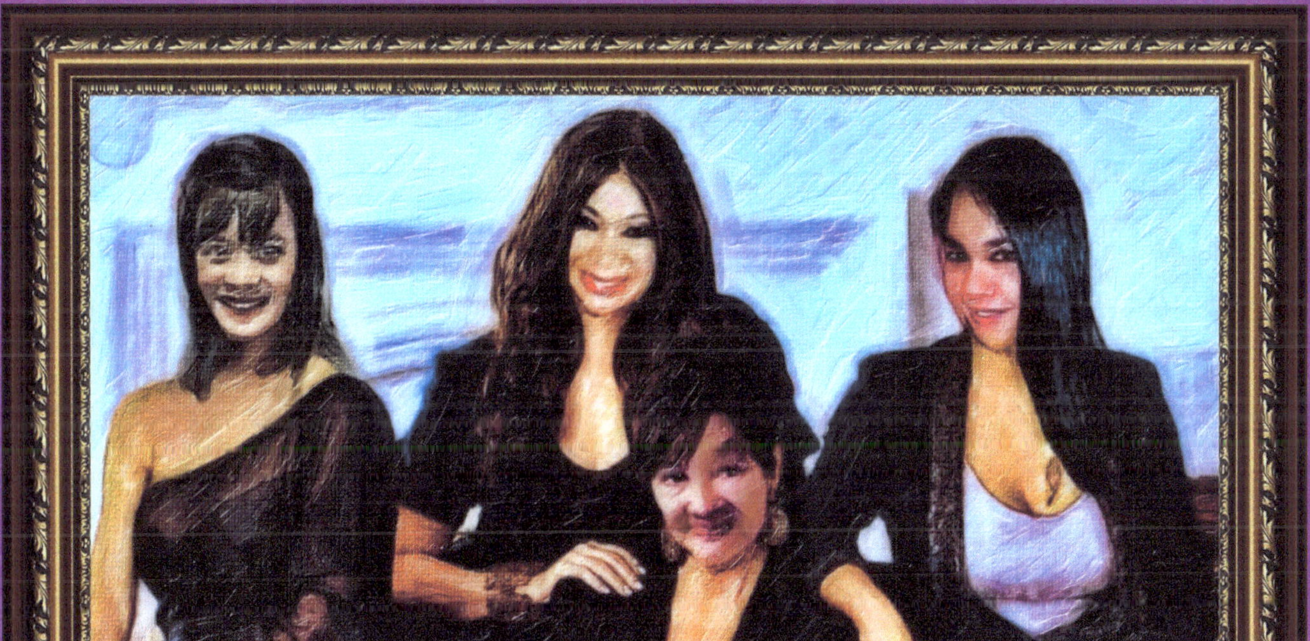

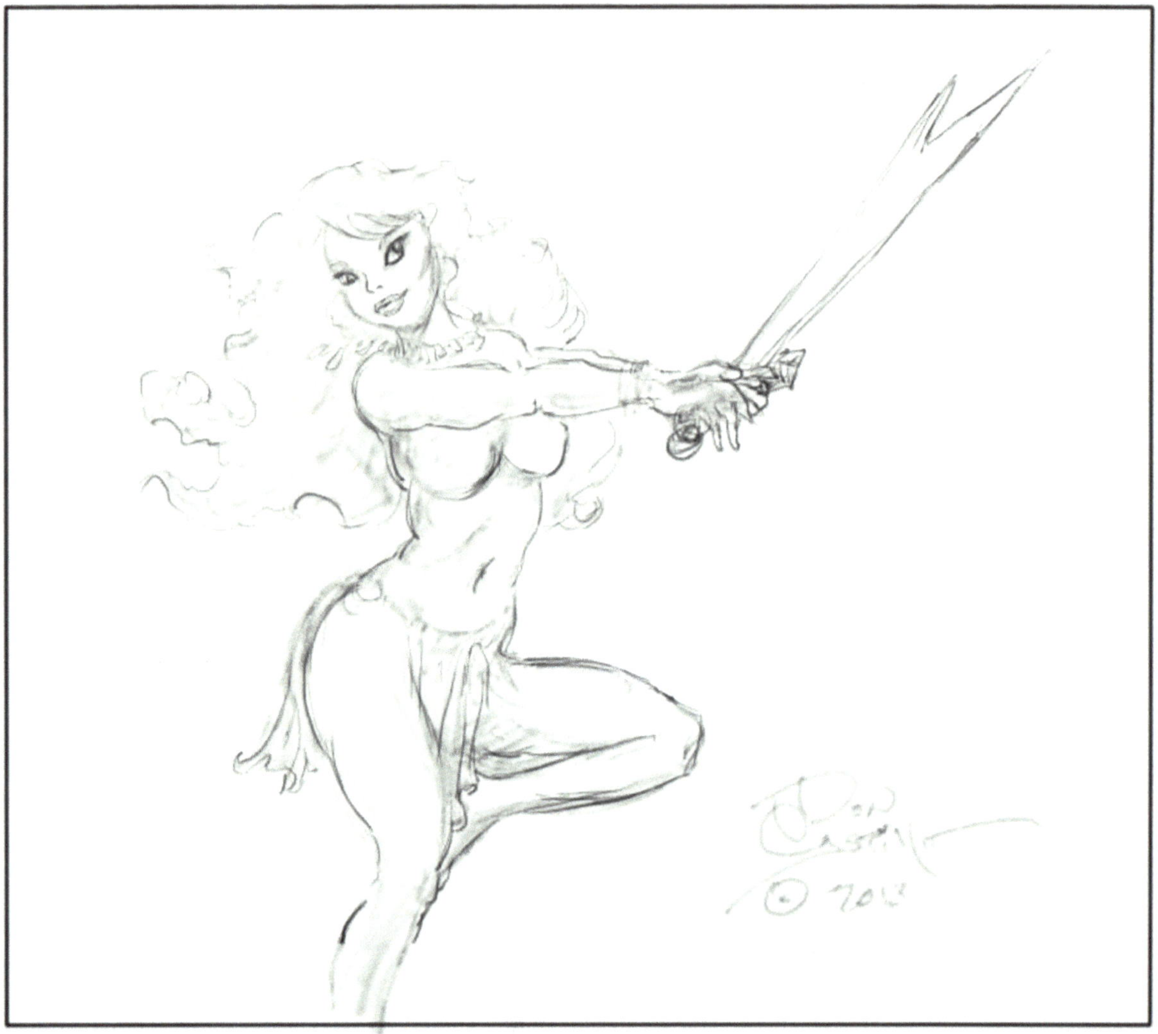

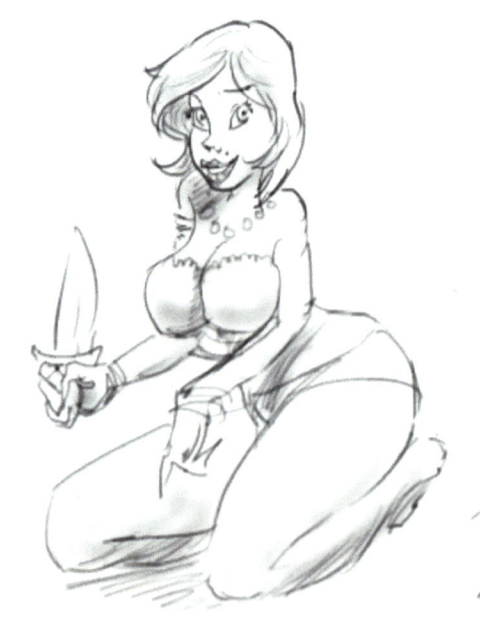

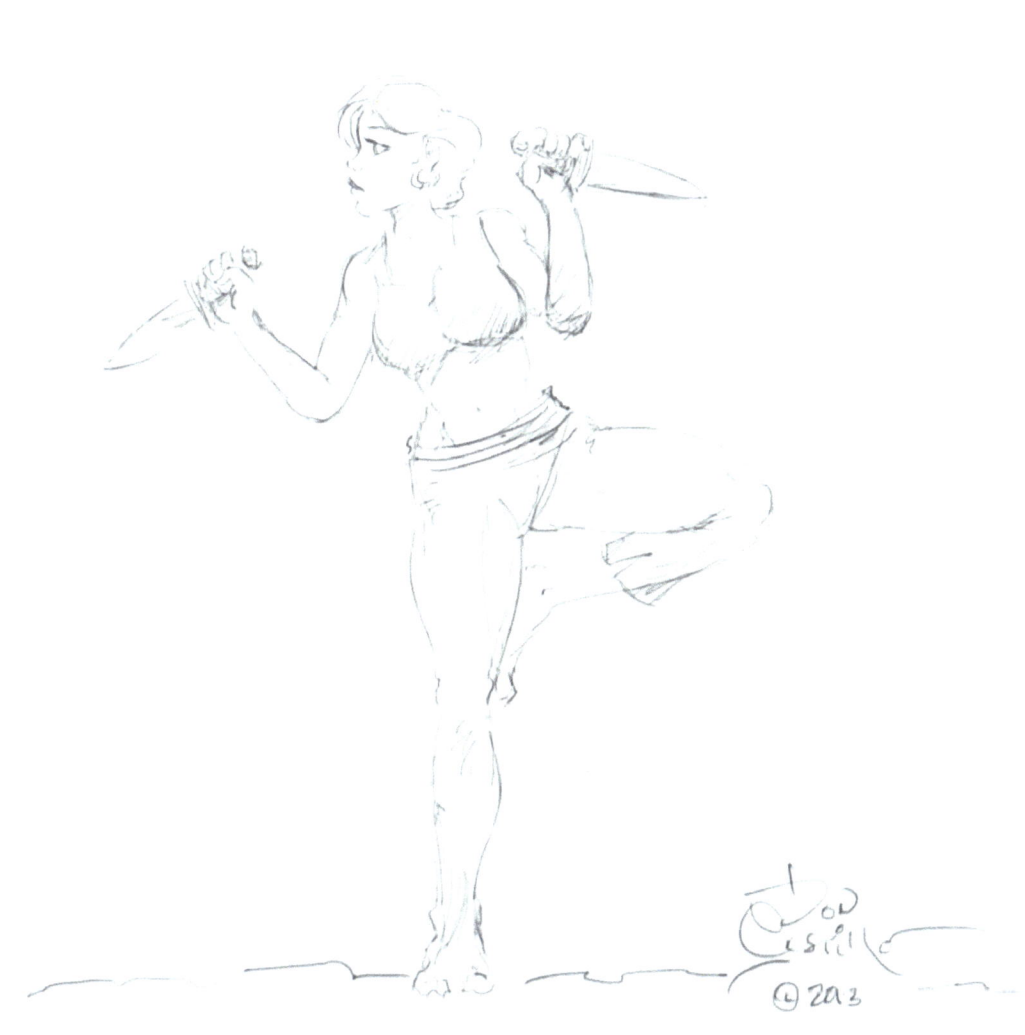

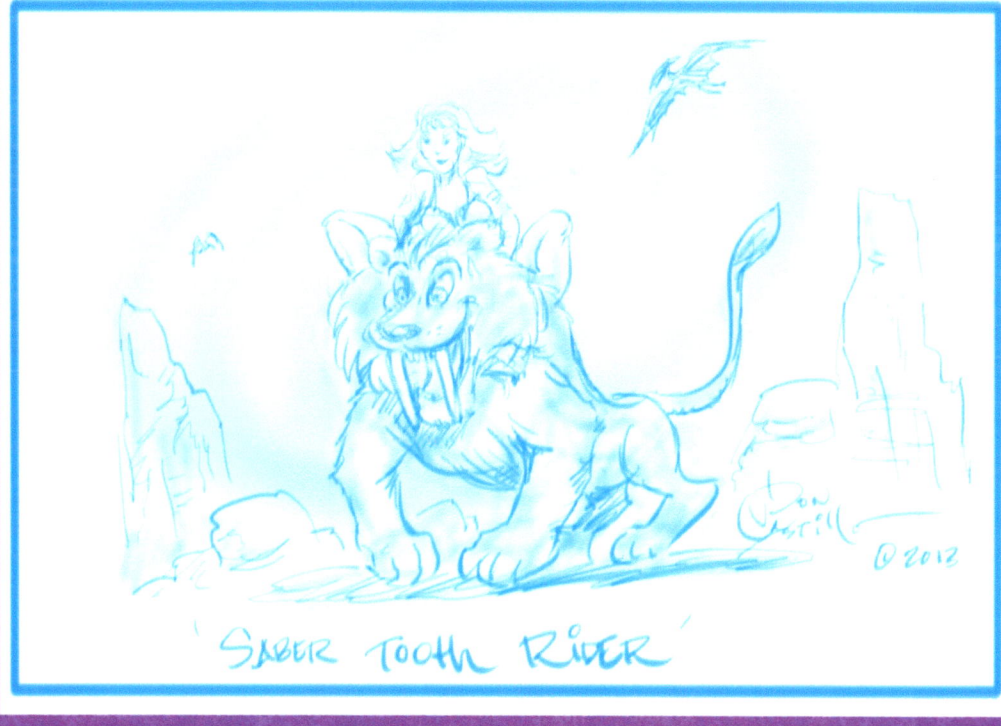

Saber Tooth Rider

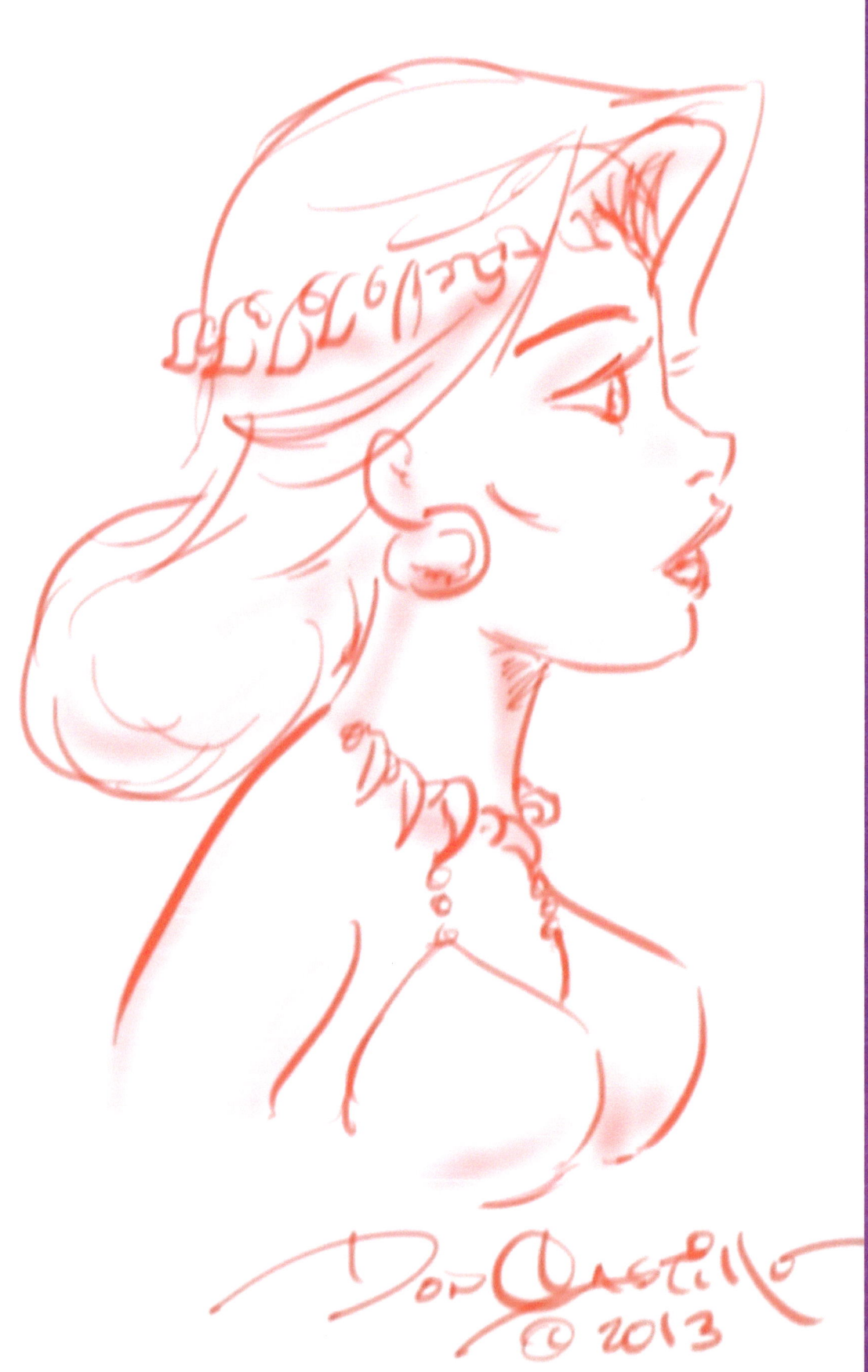

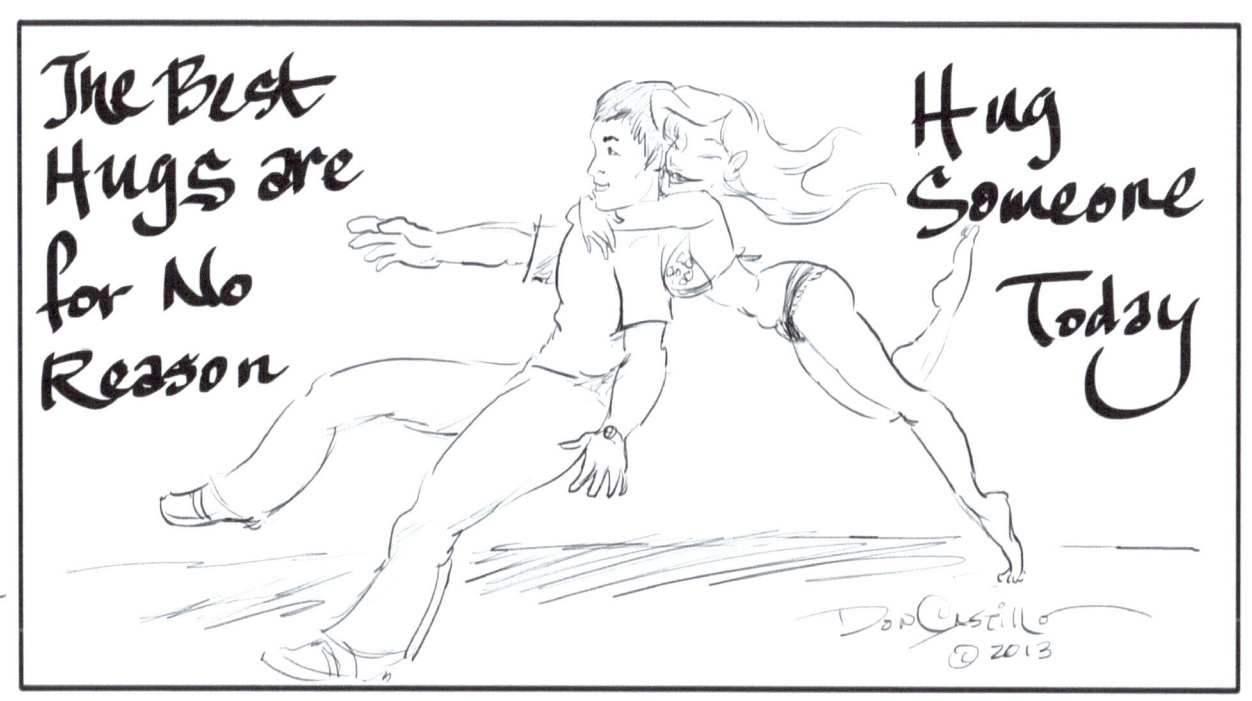

The Best Hugs are for No Reason

Hug Someone Today

DonCastillo © 2013

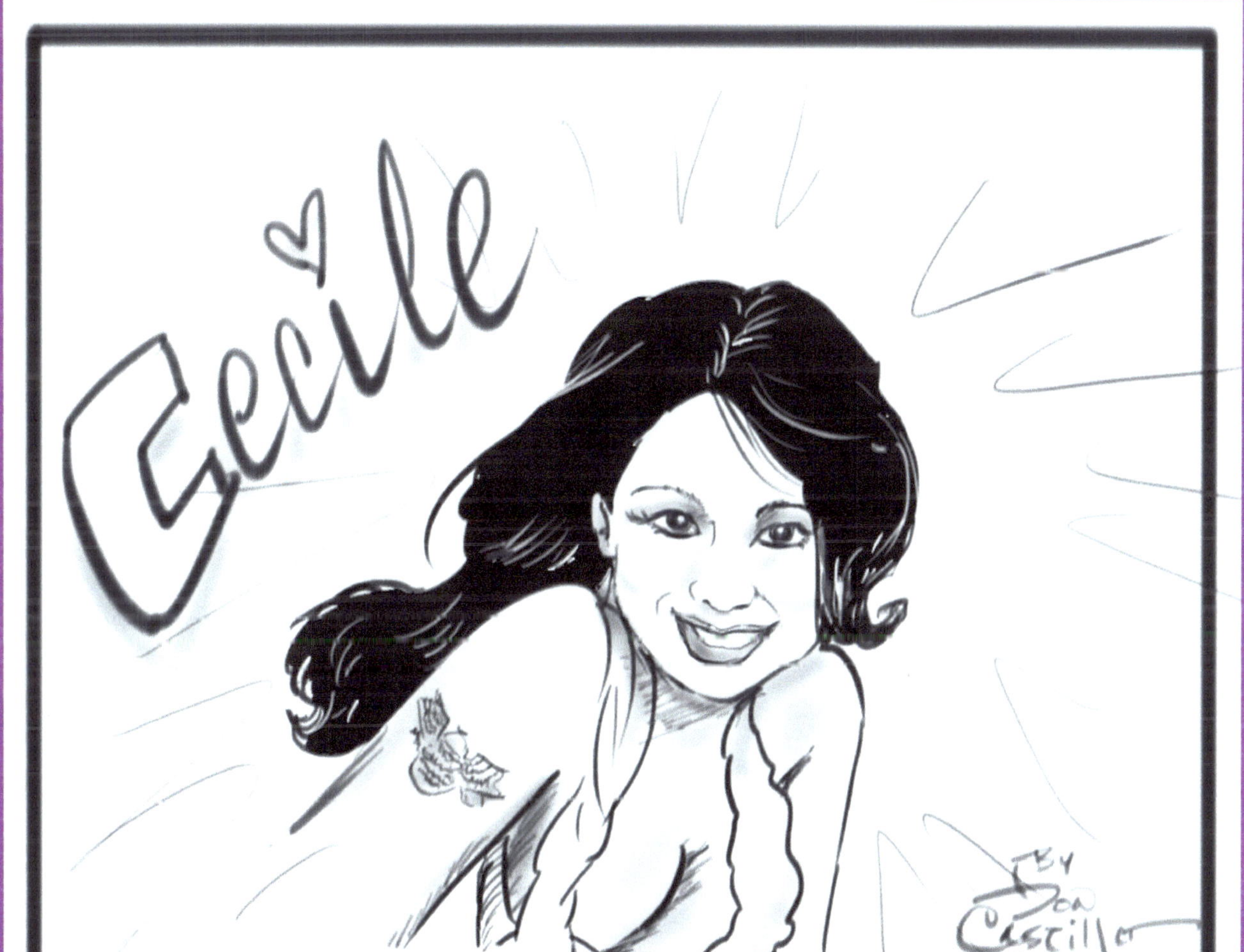

Cecile

By Don Castillo

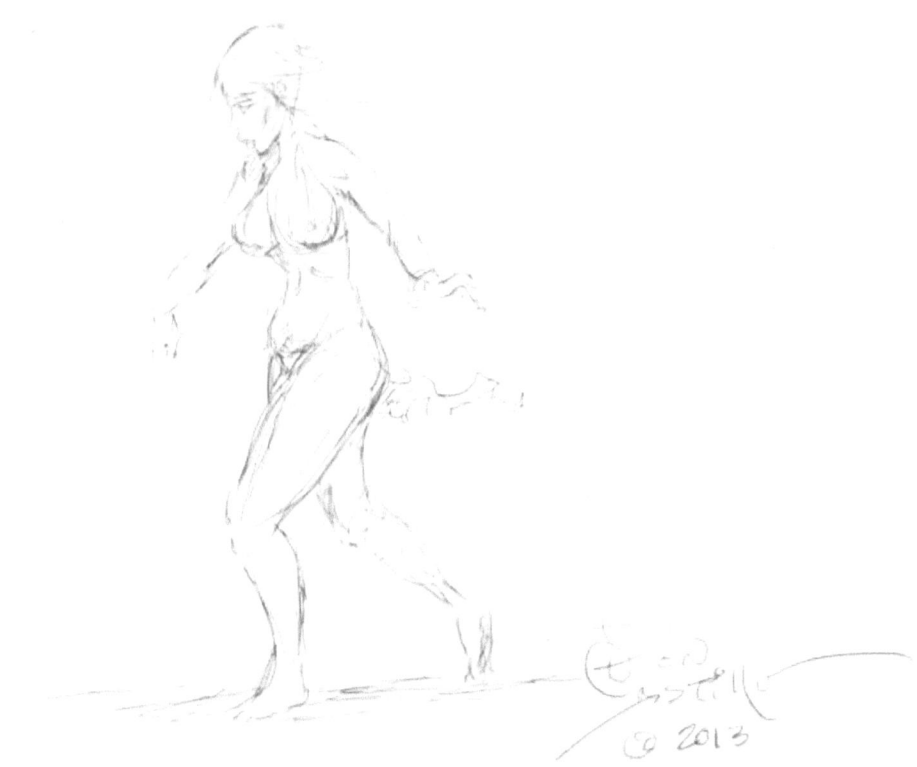

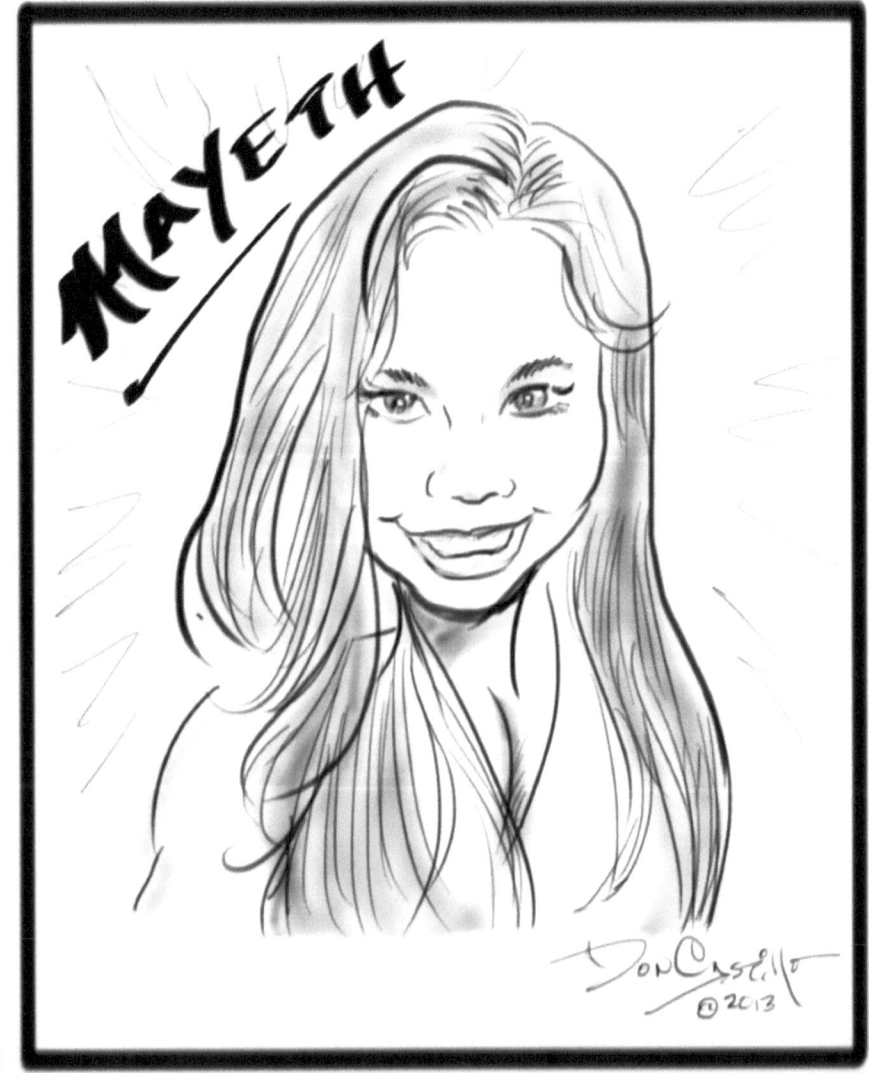

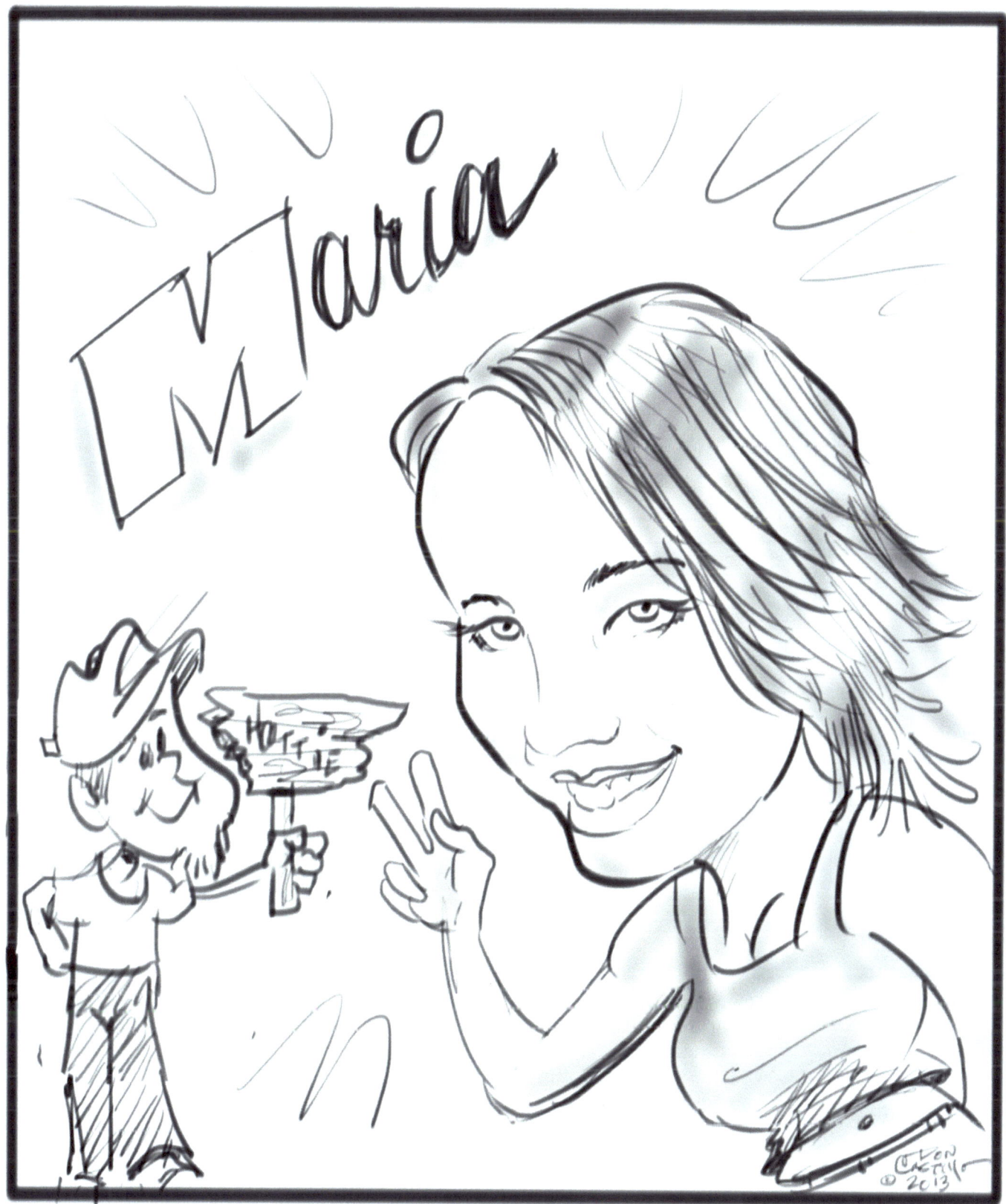

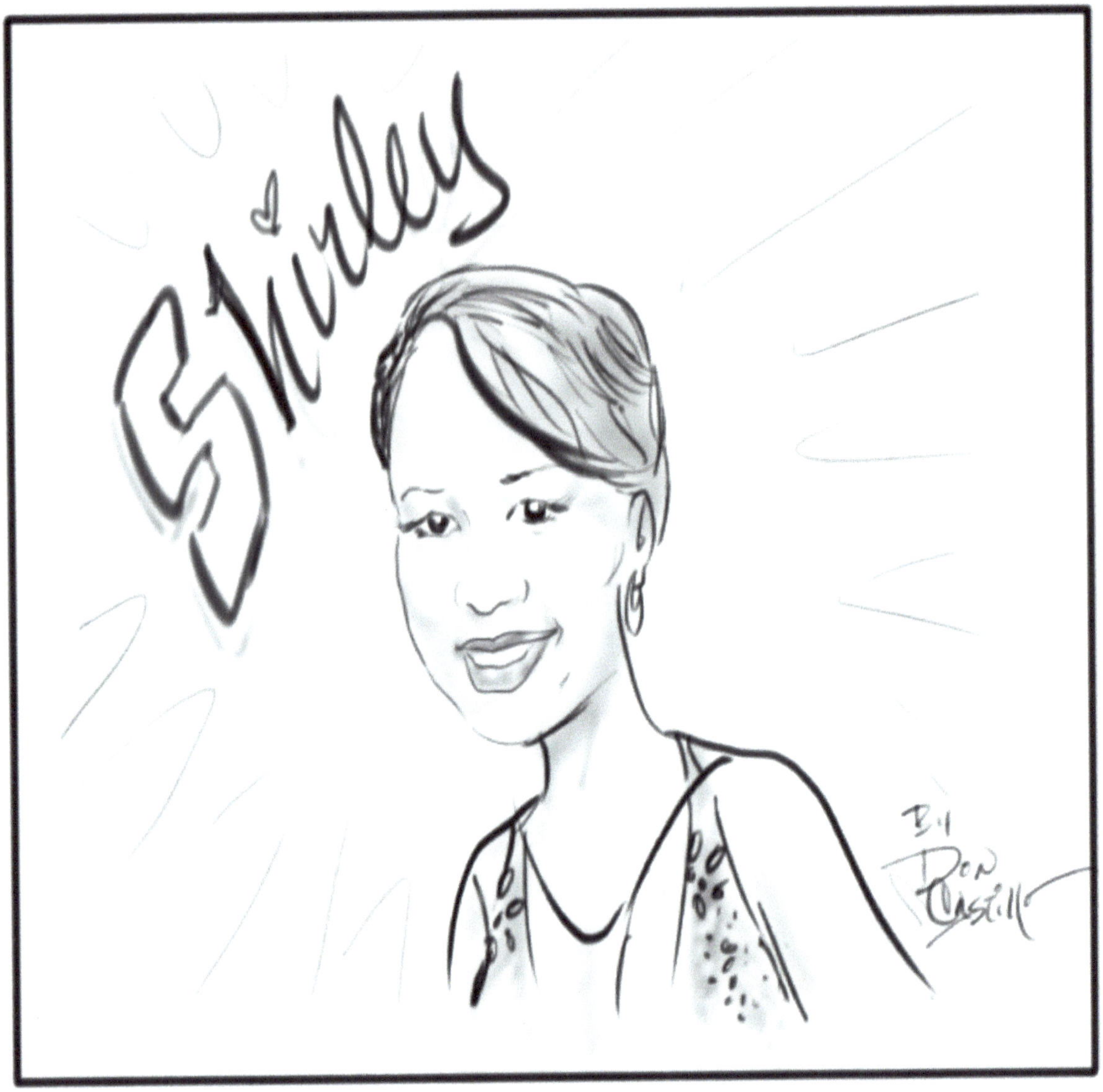

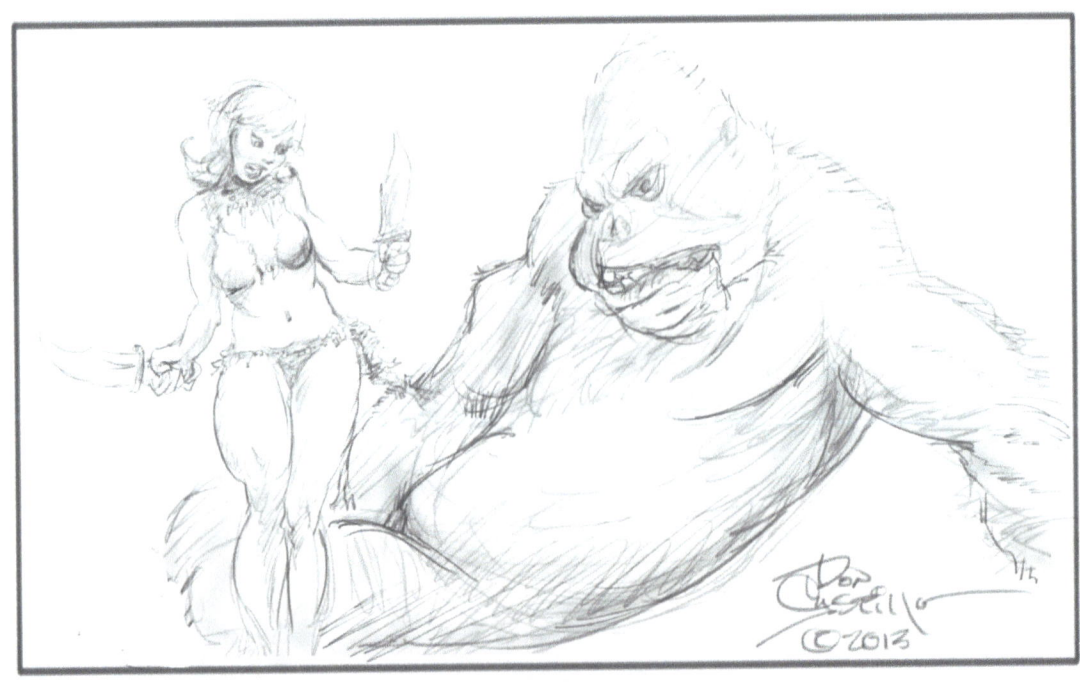

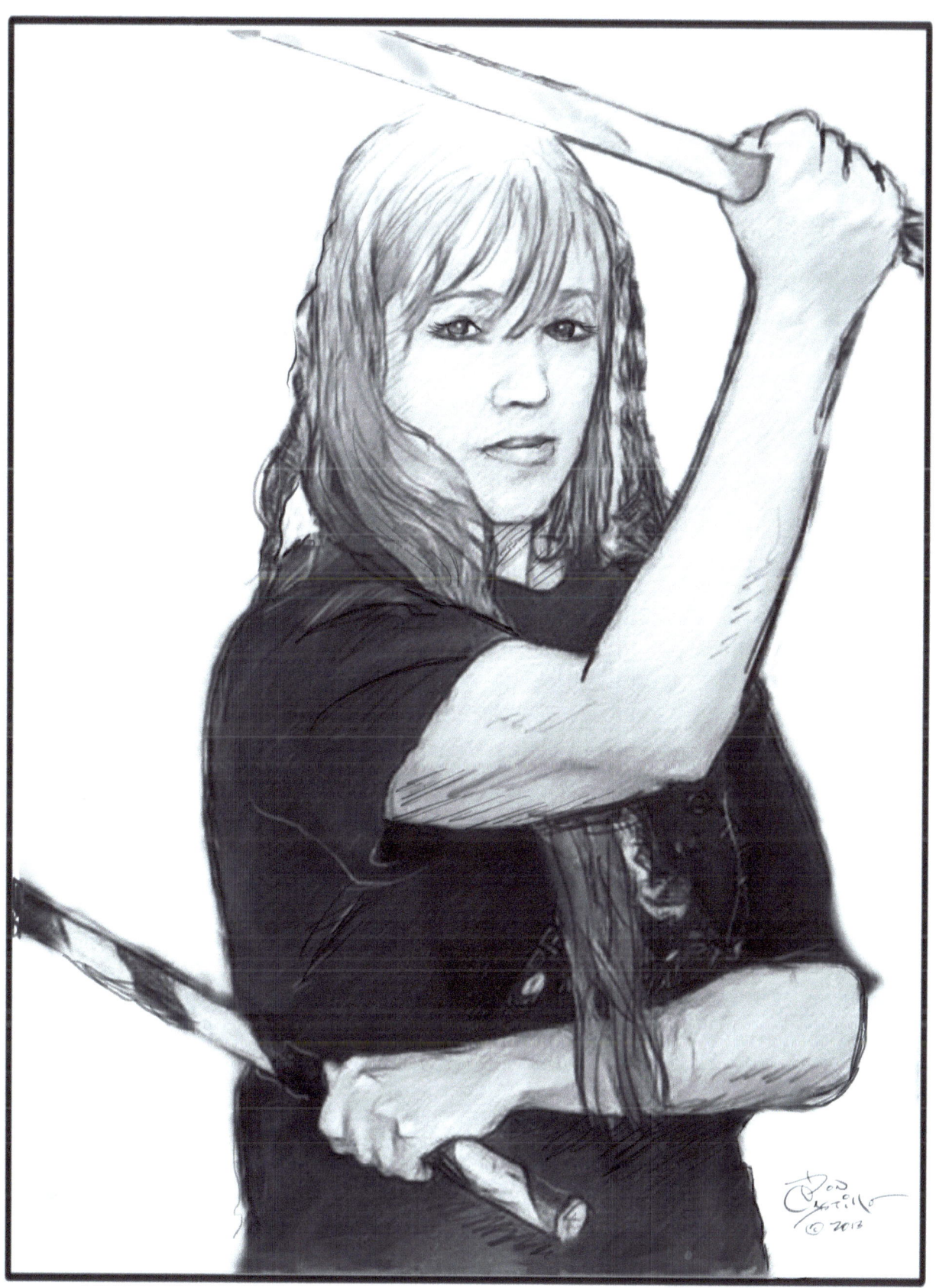

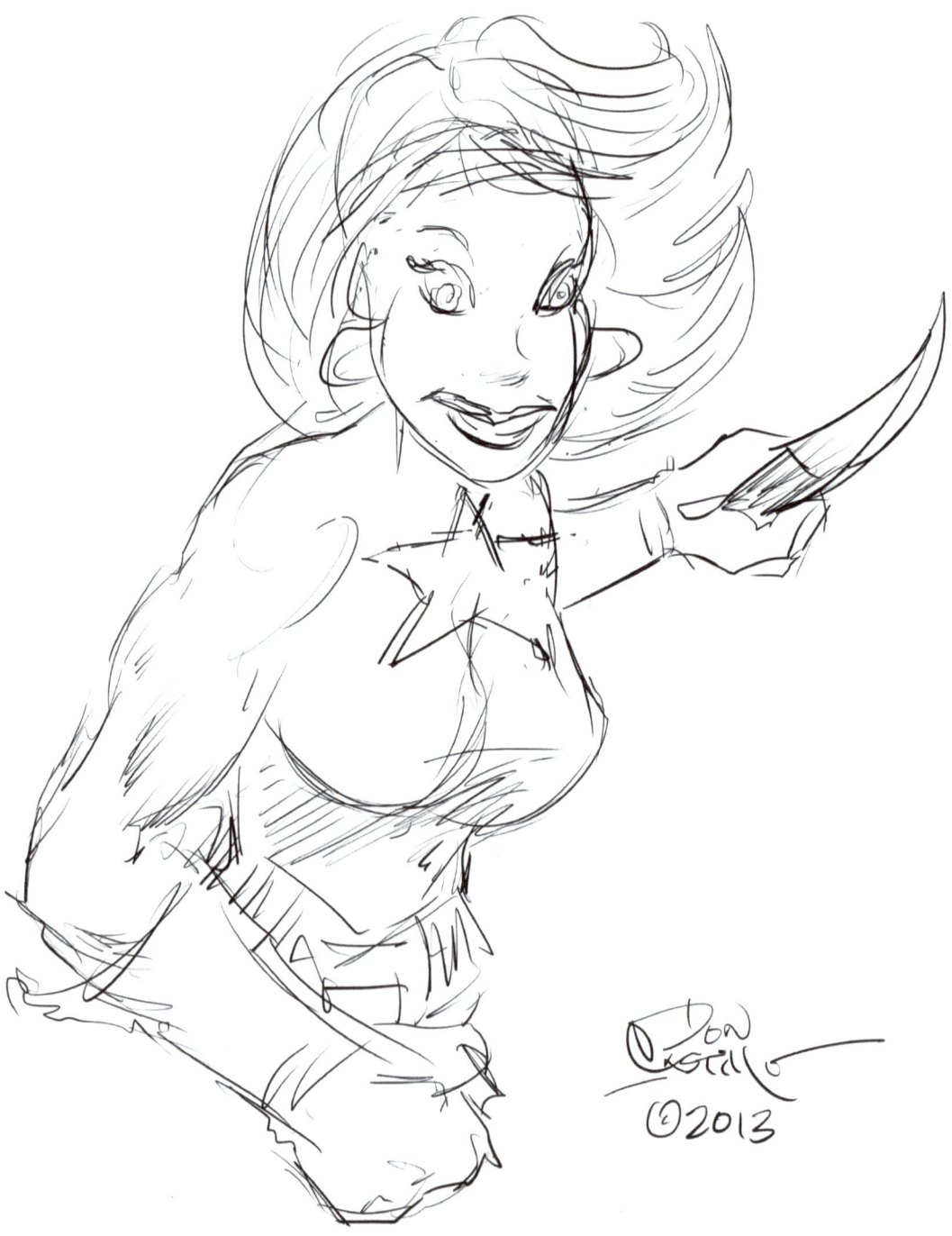

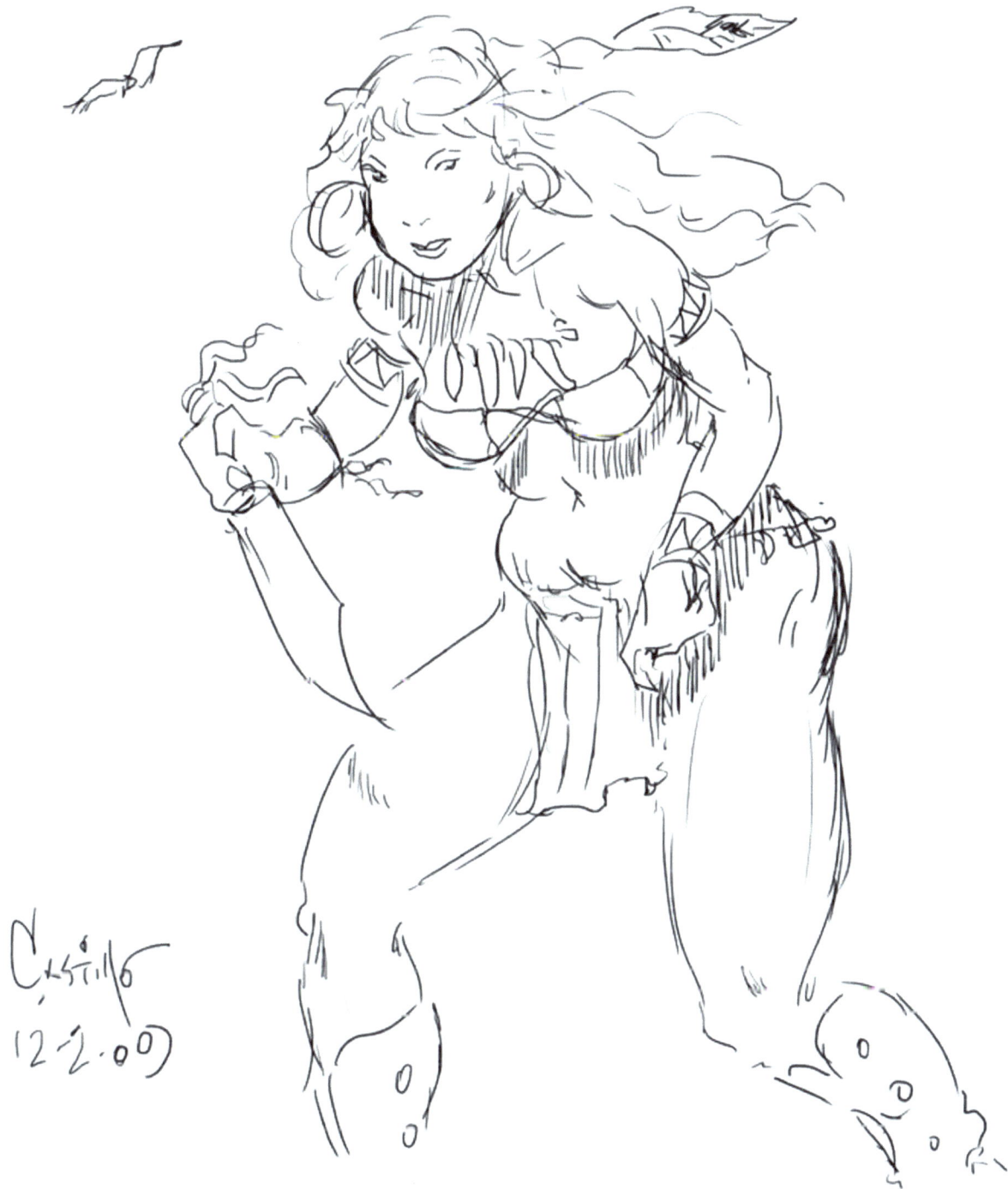

MARTIAL ARTS FOR LIFE!

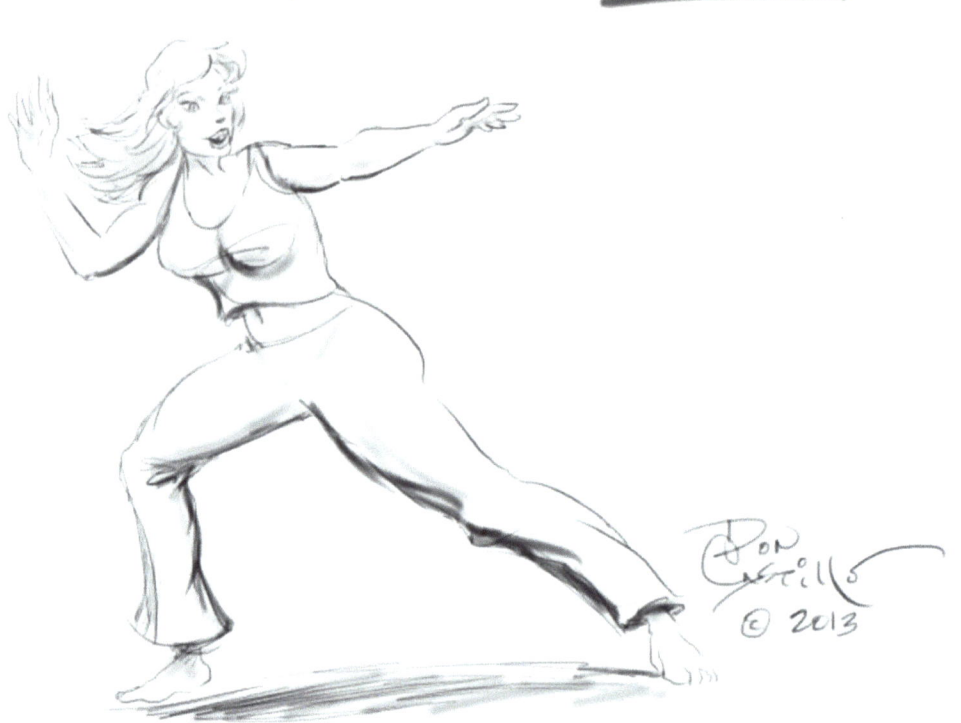

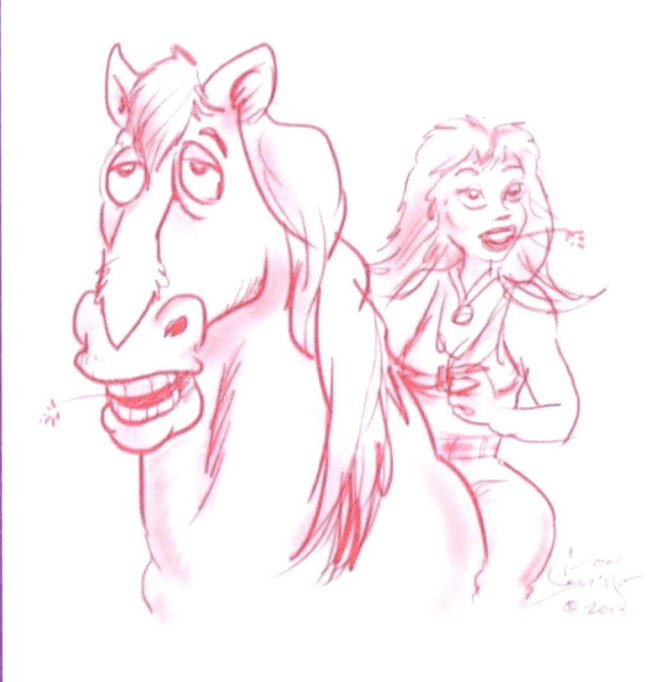

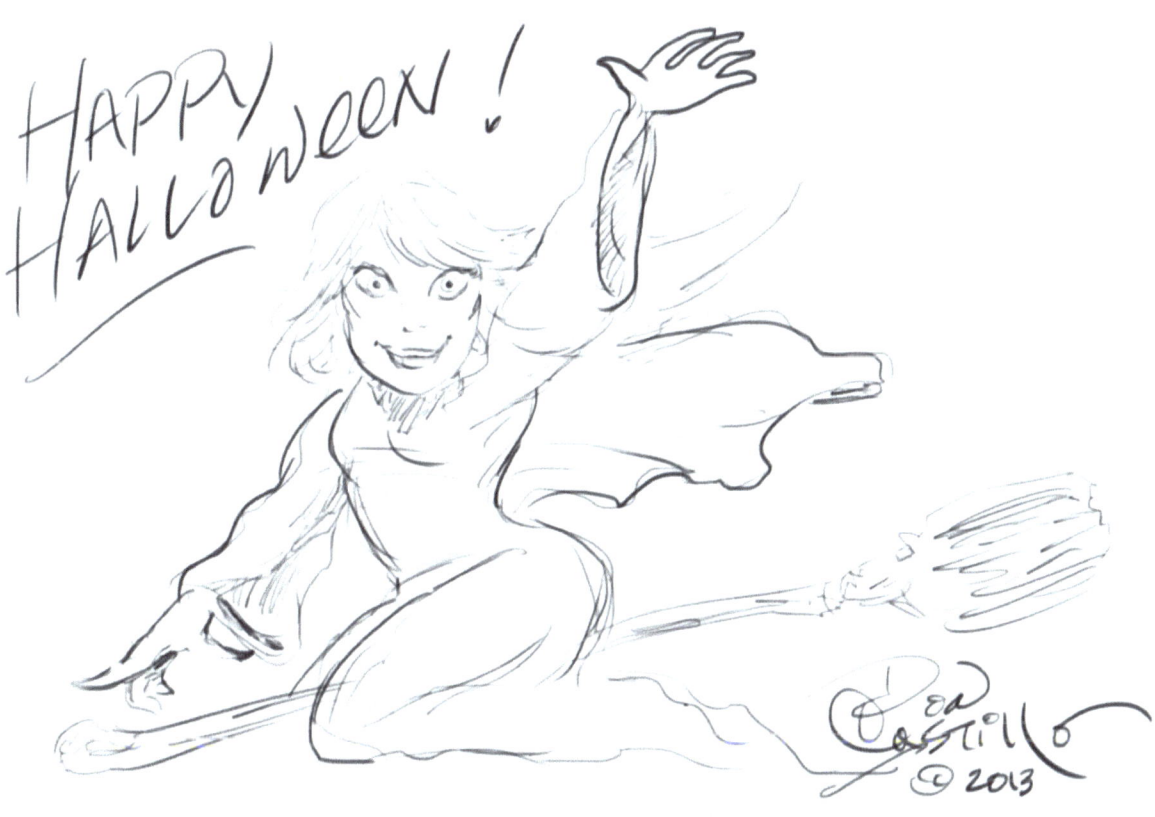

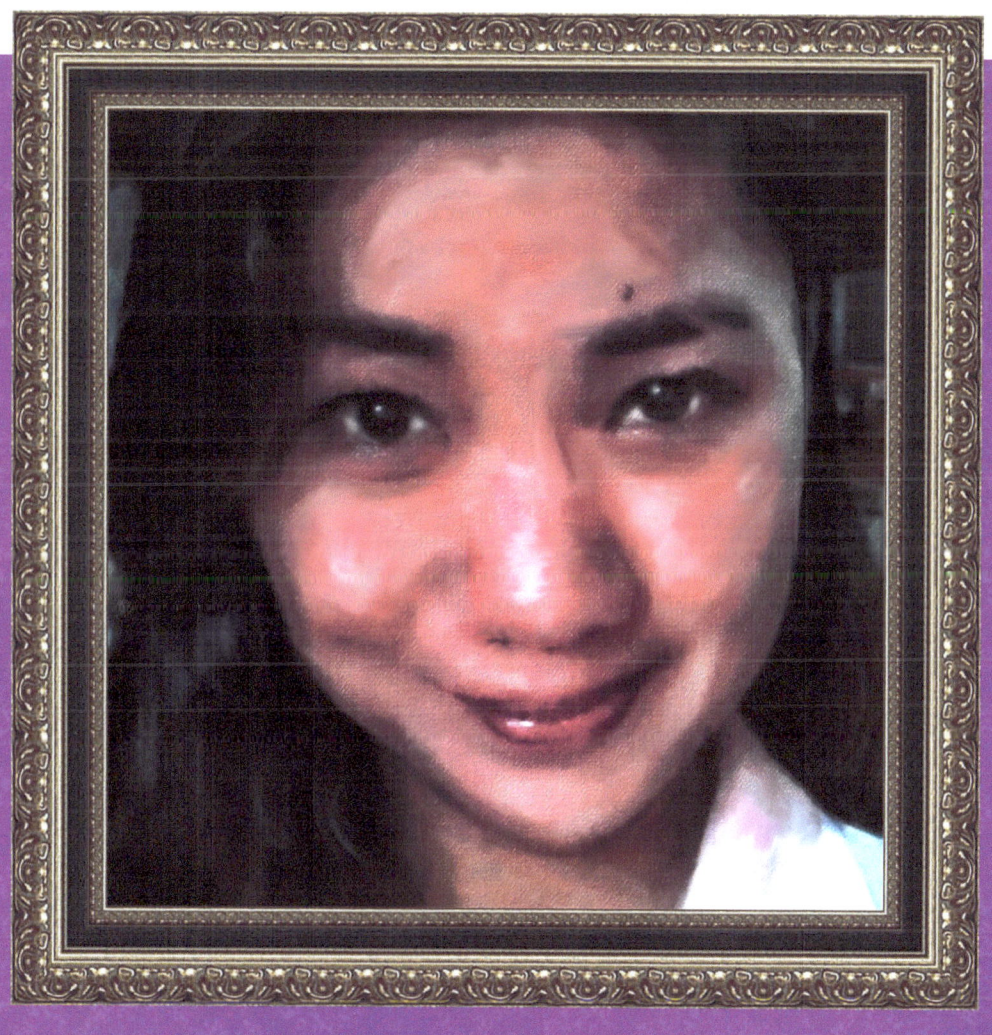

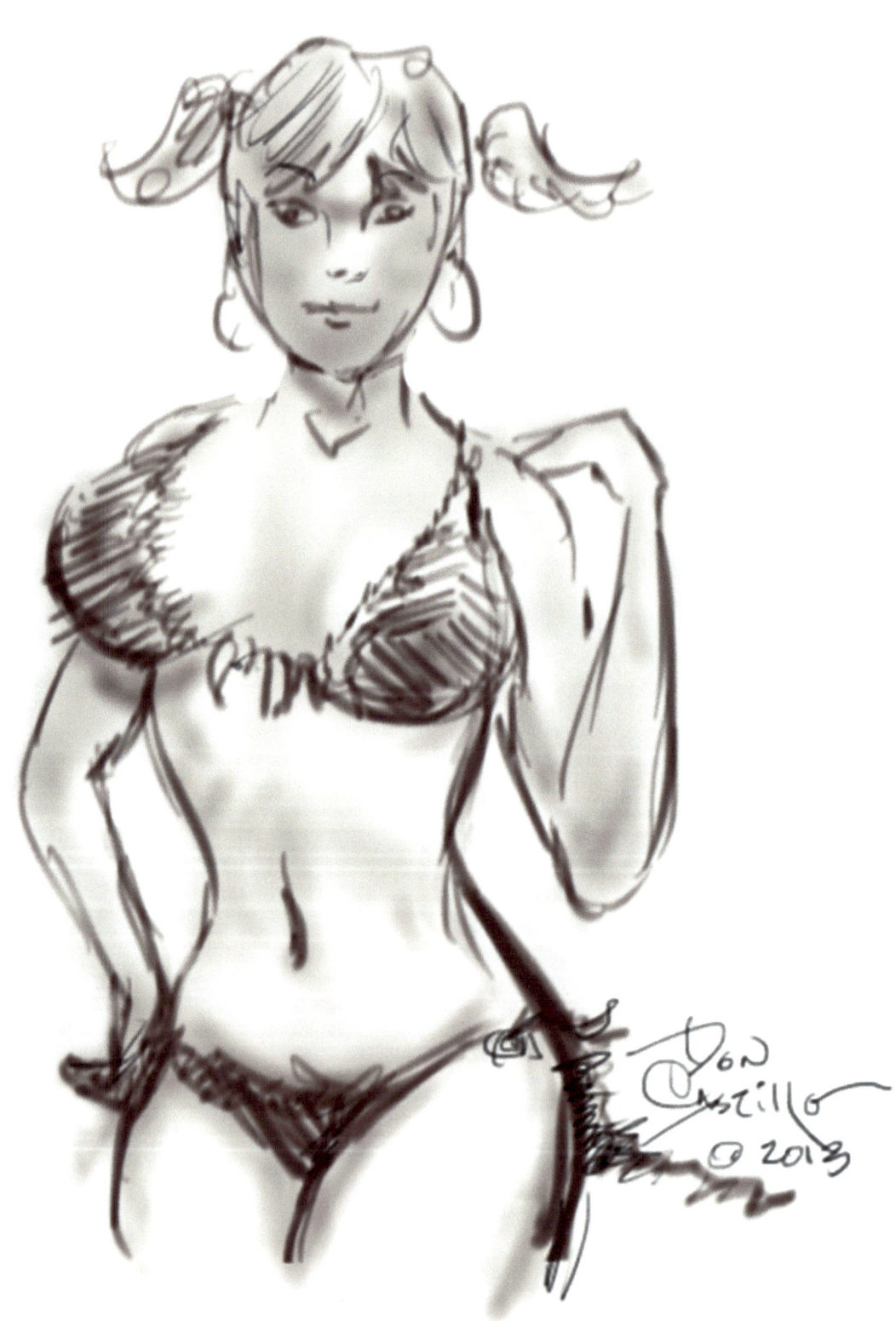

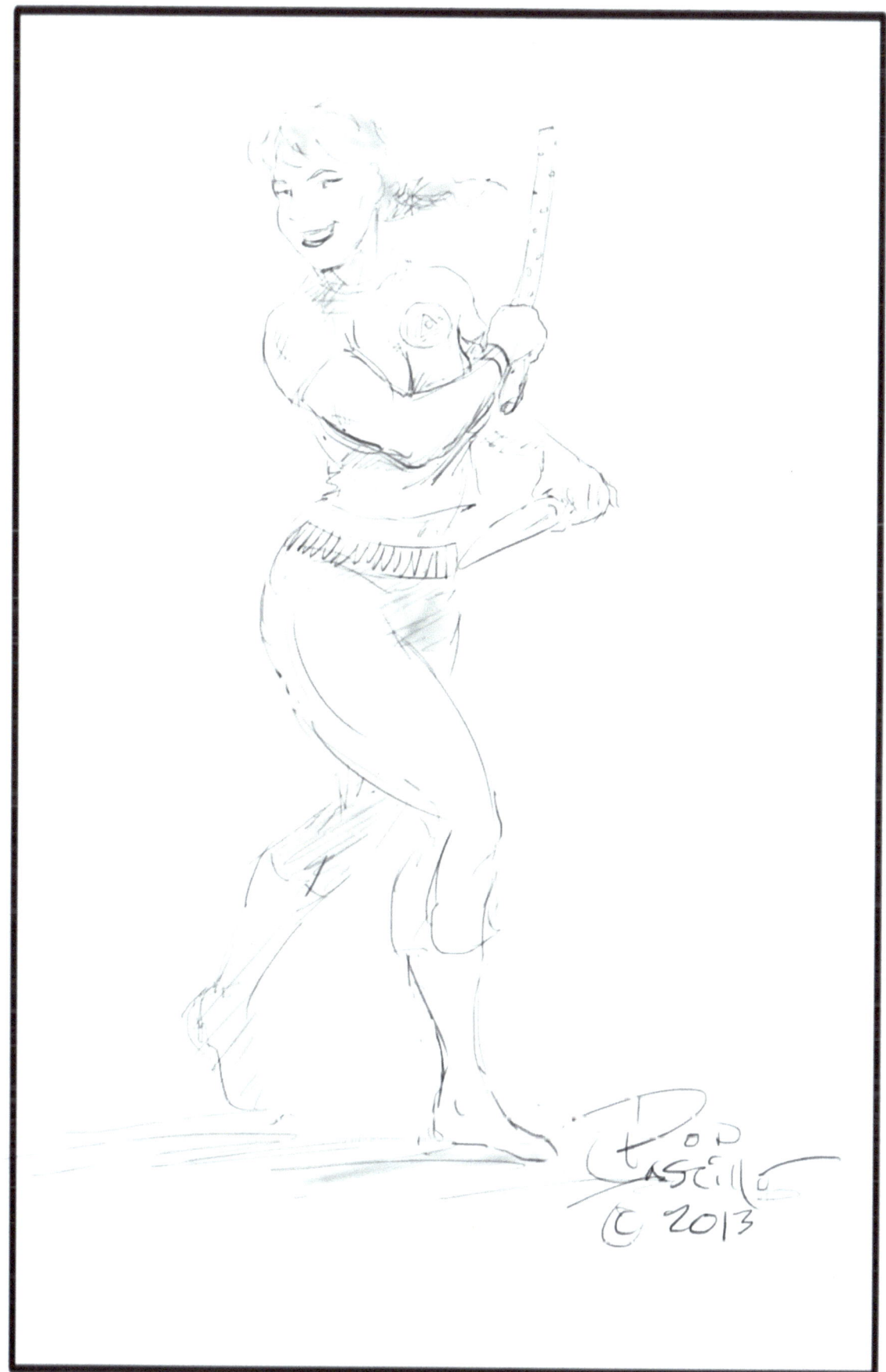

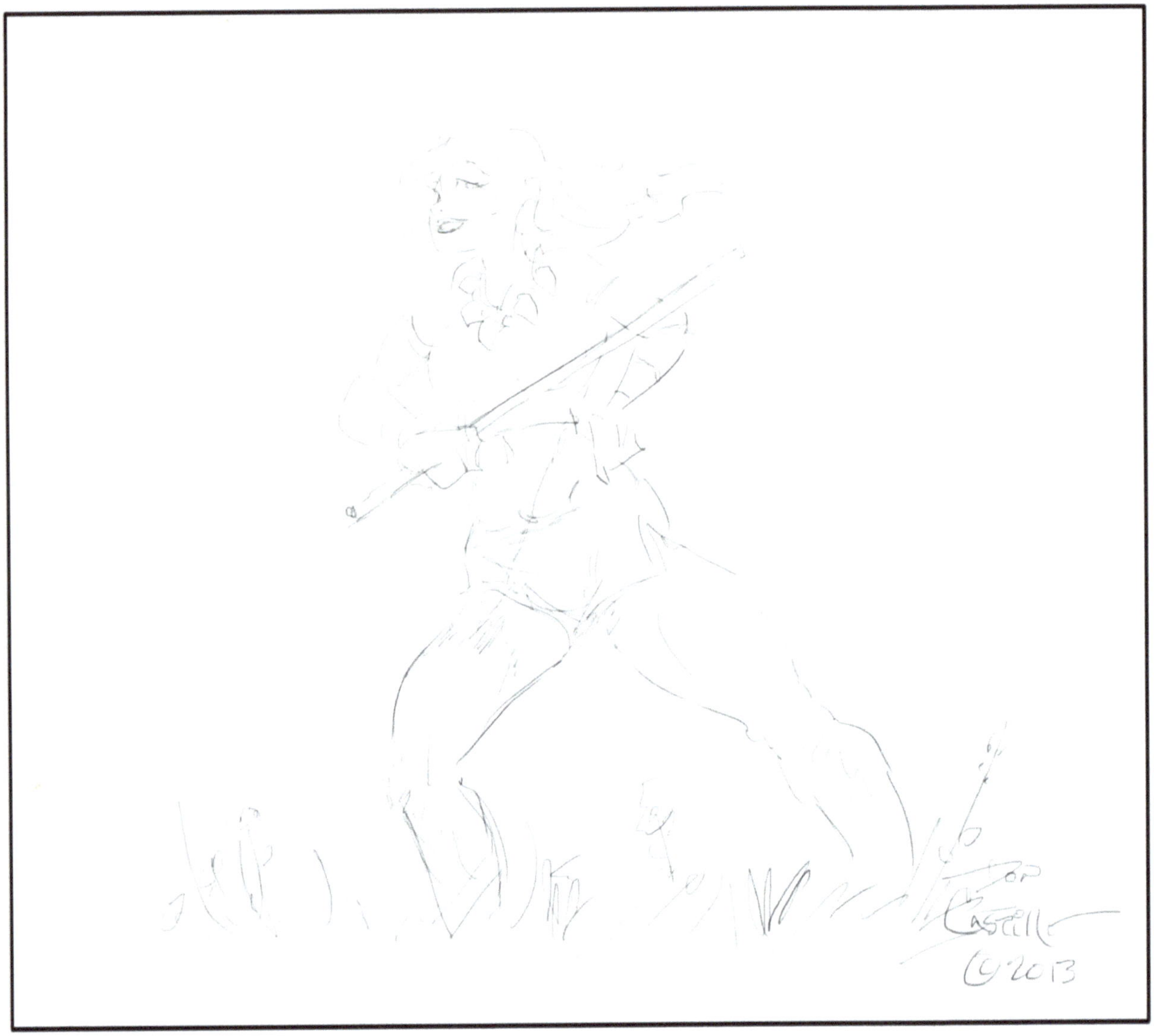

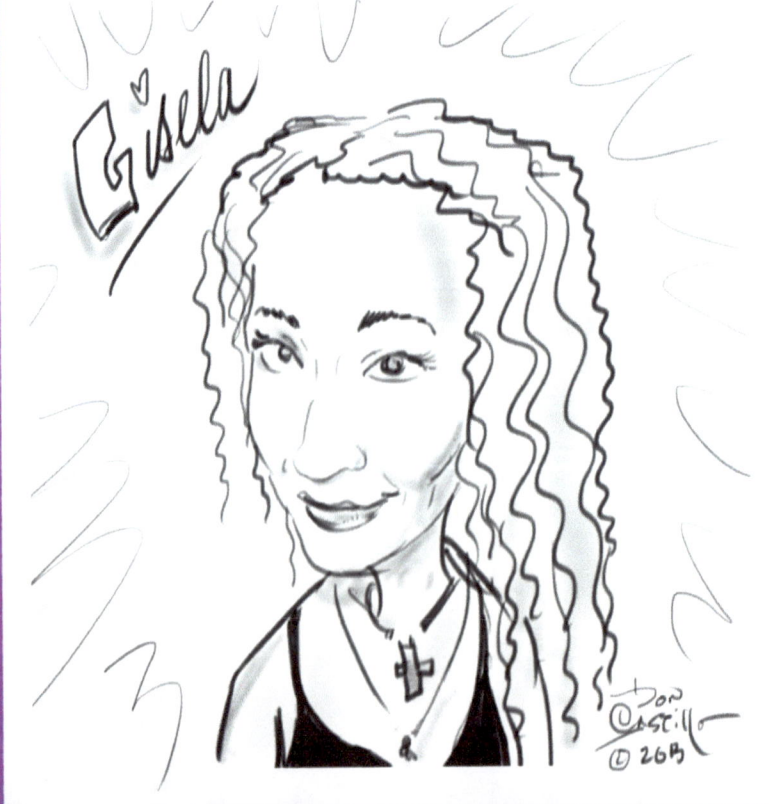

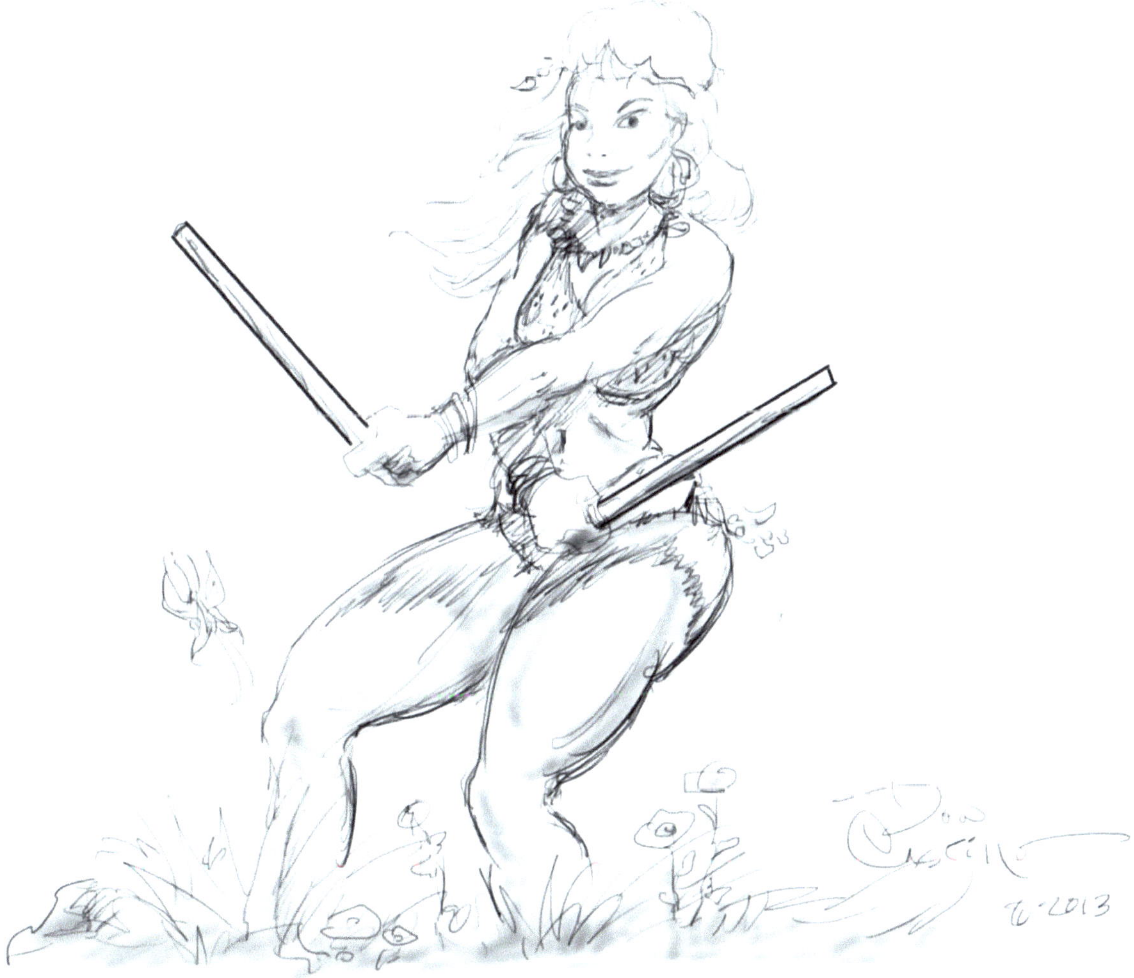

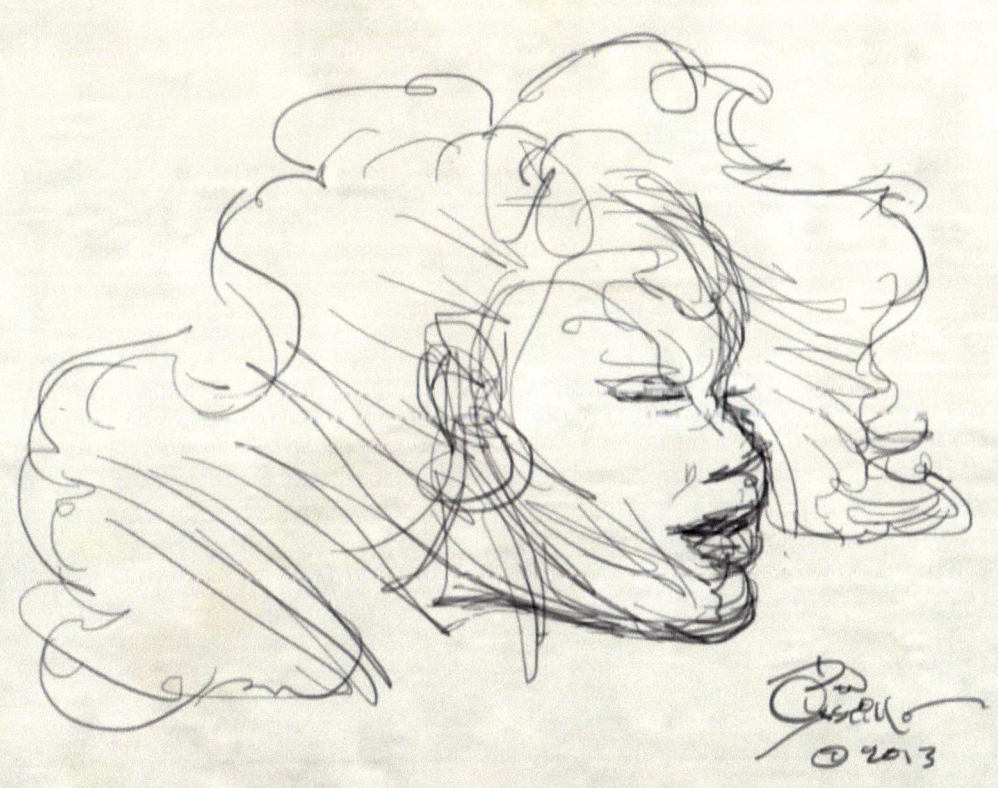

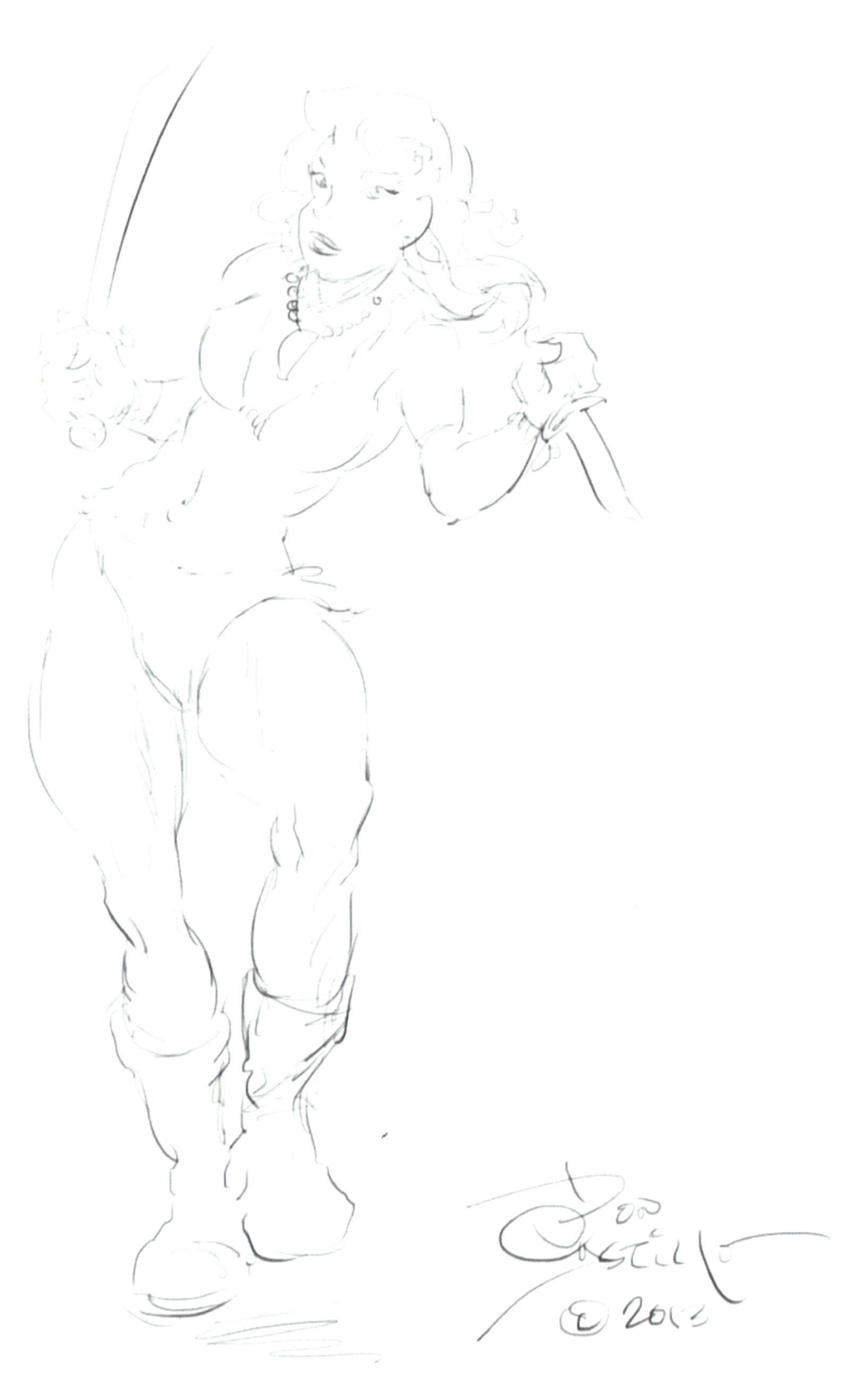

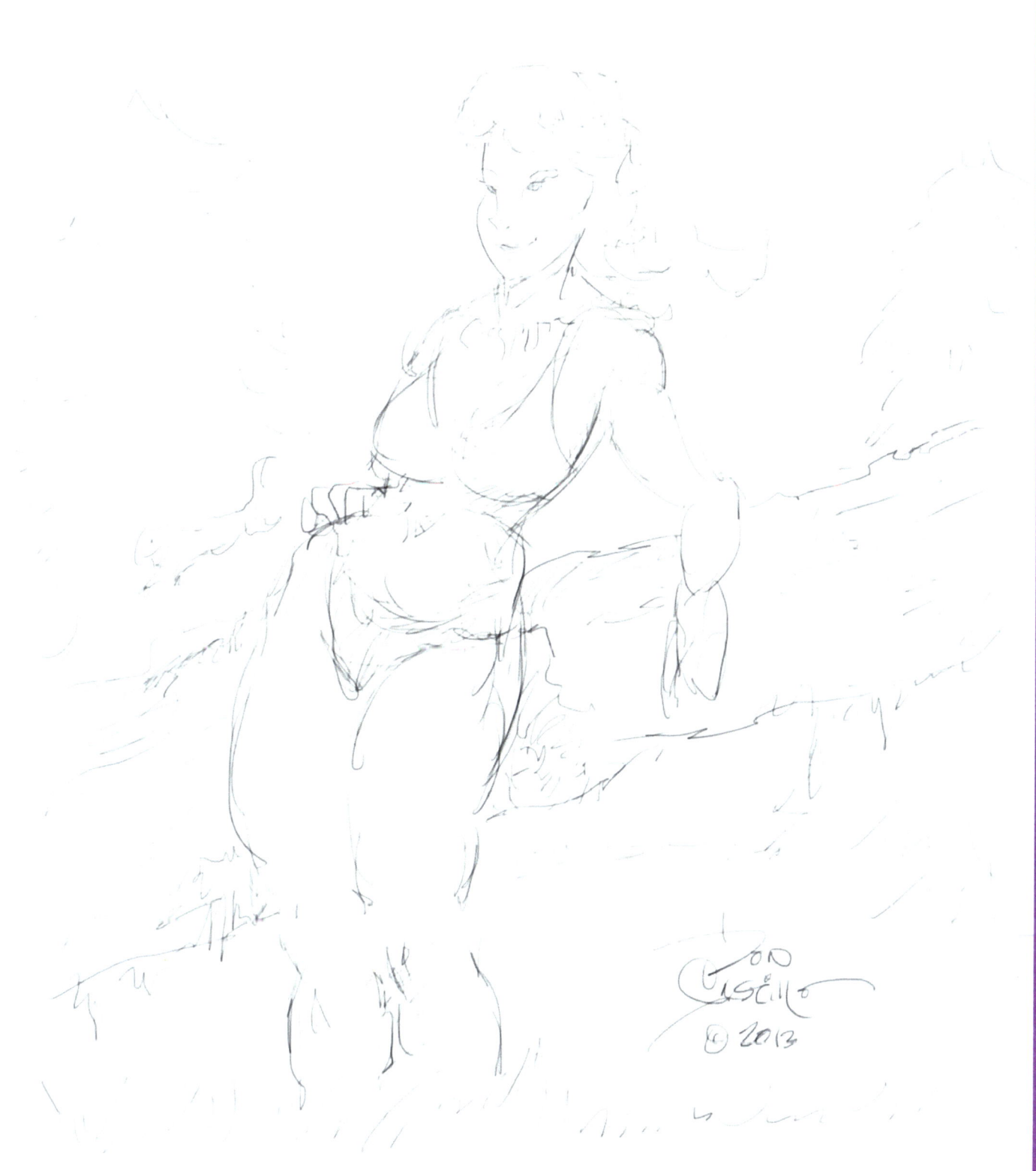

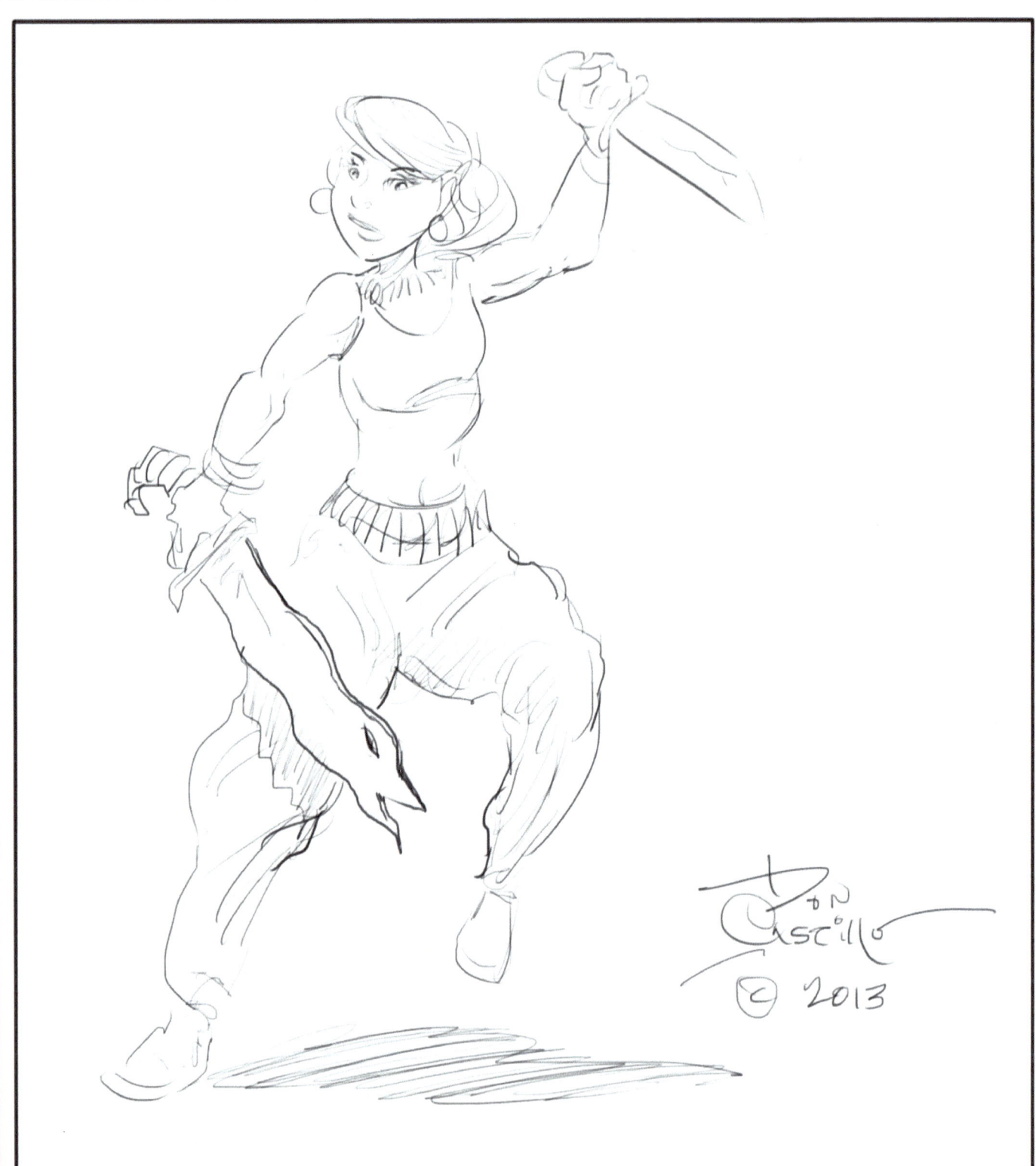

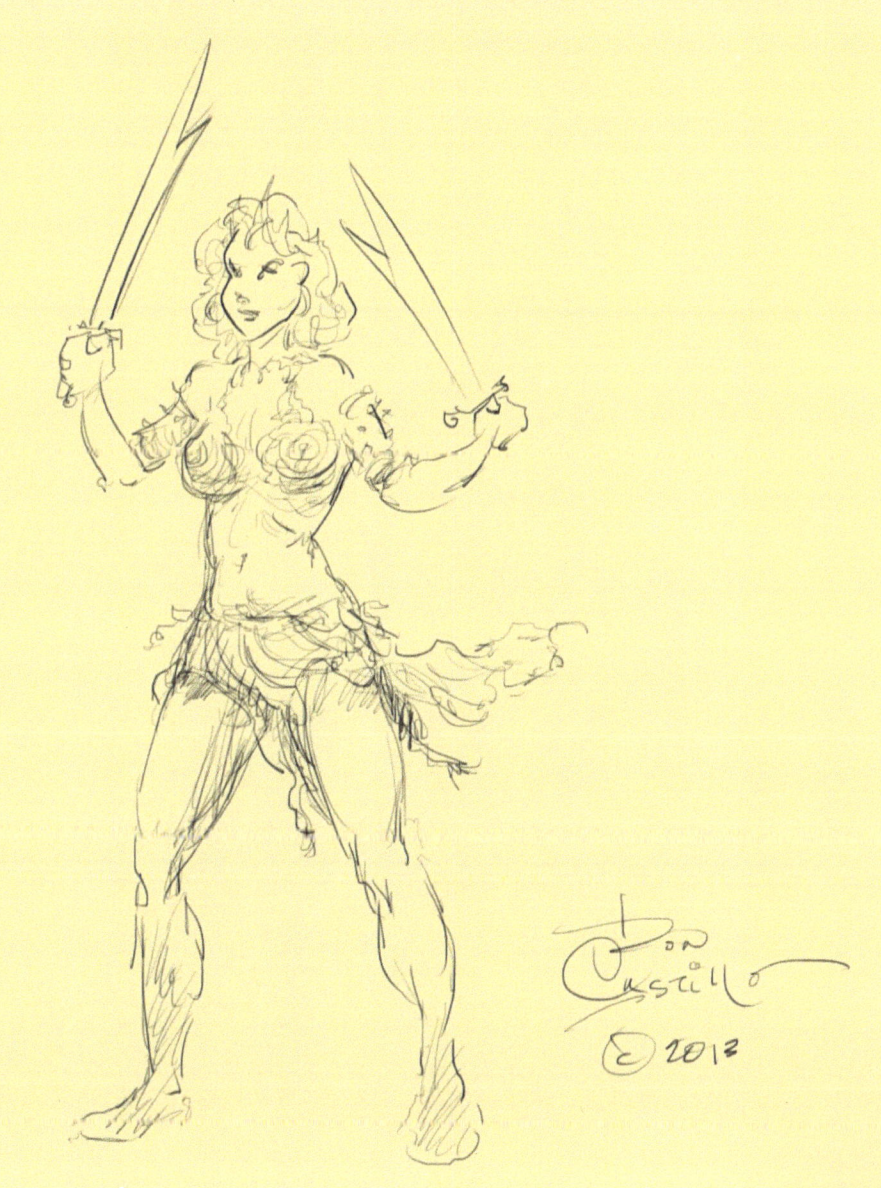

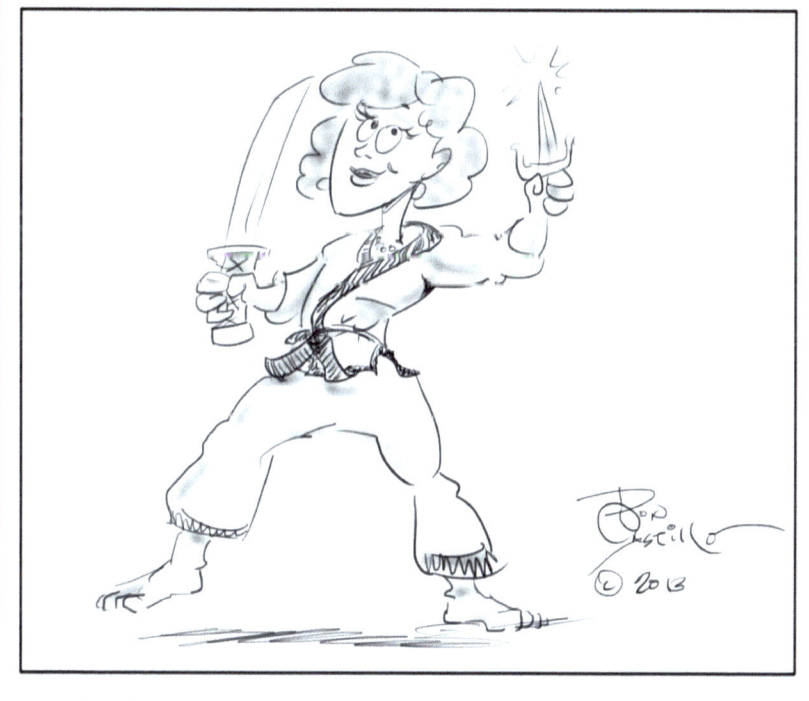

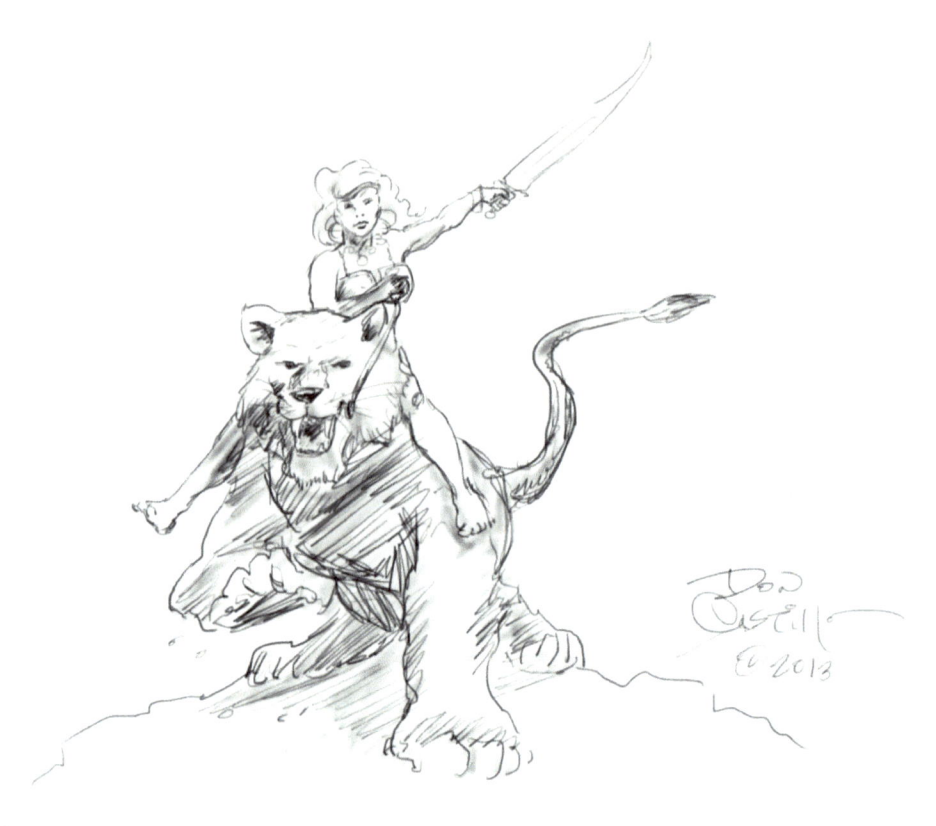
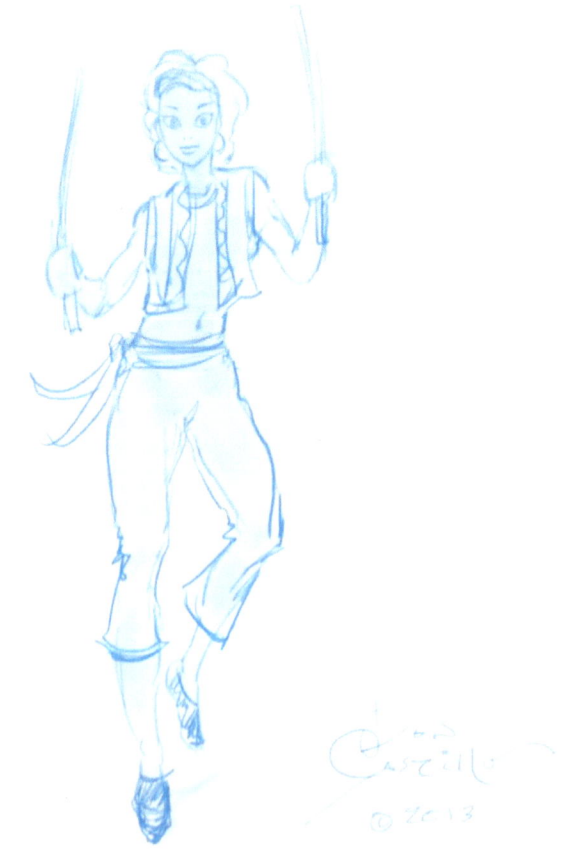

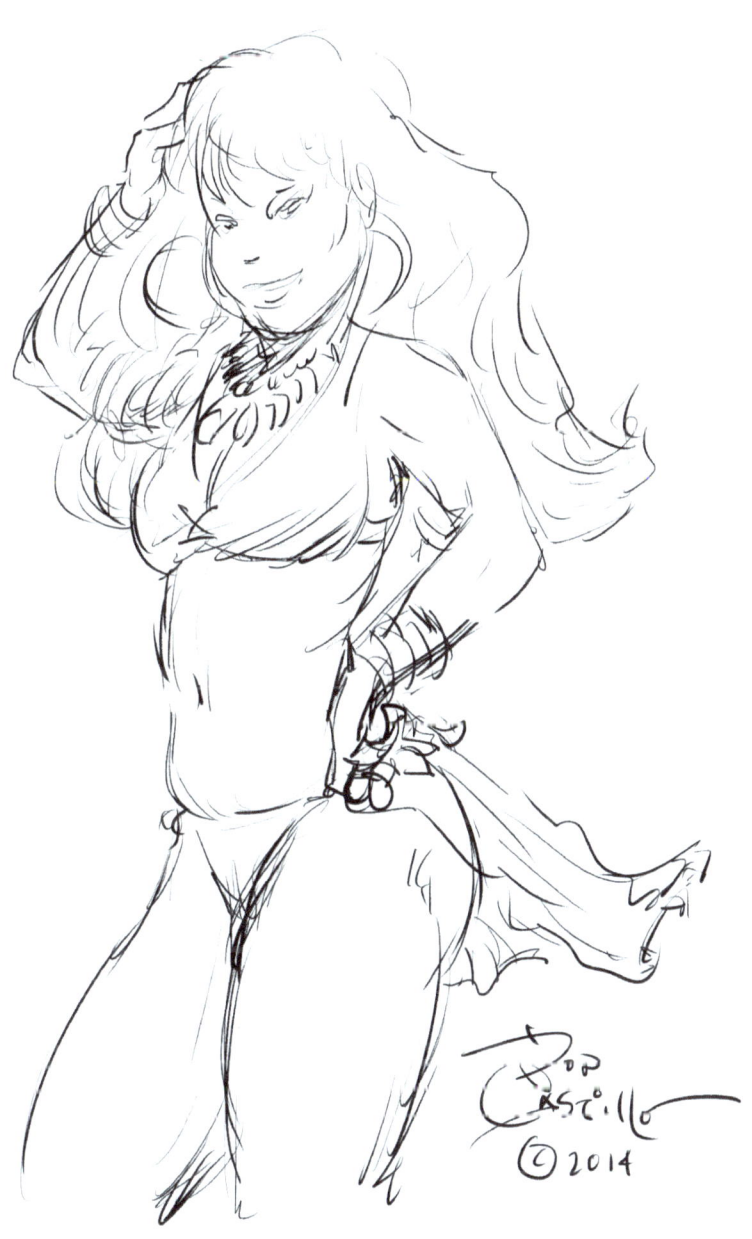

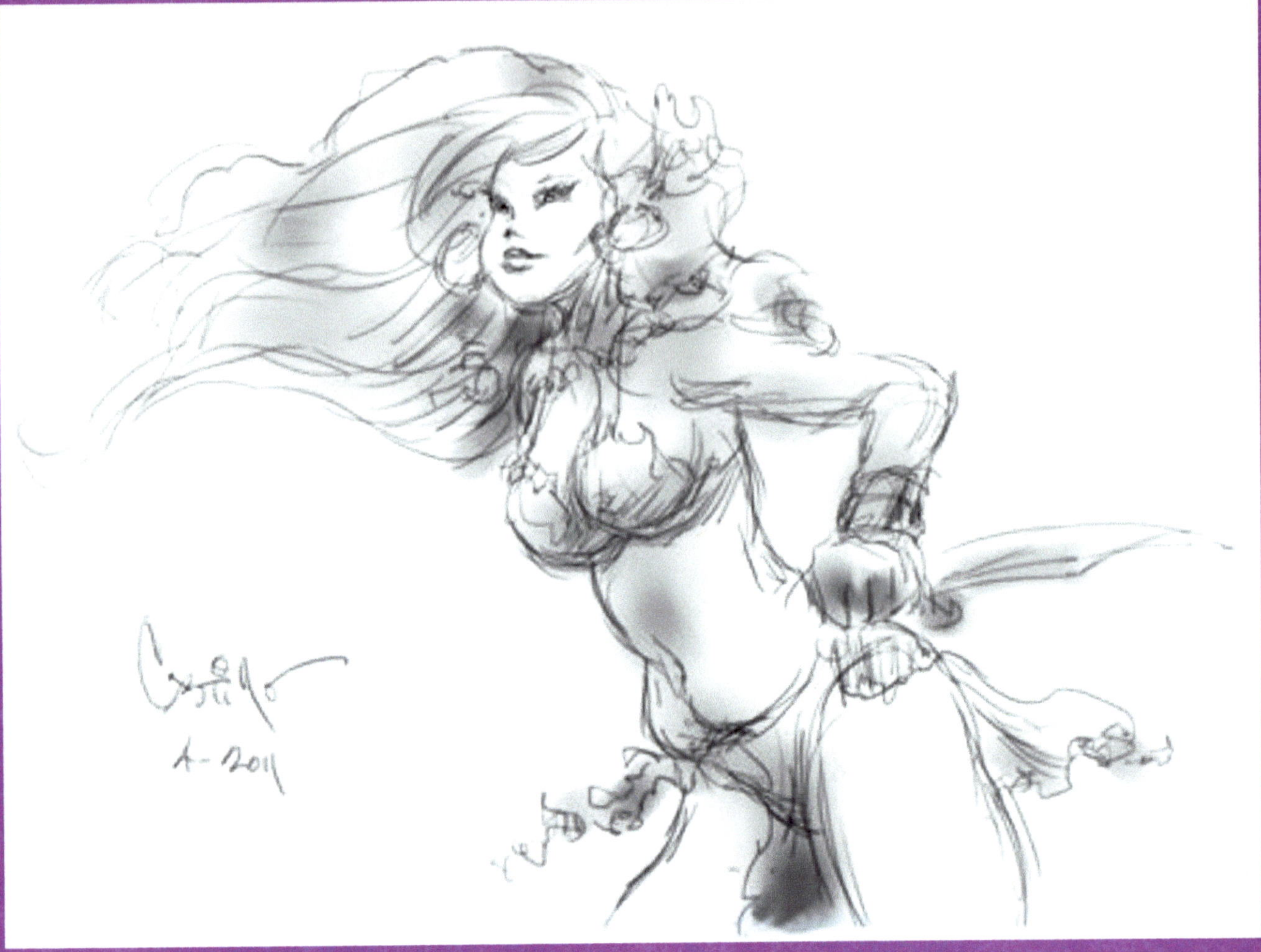

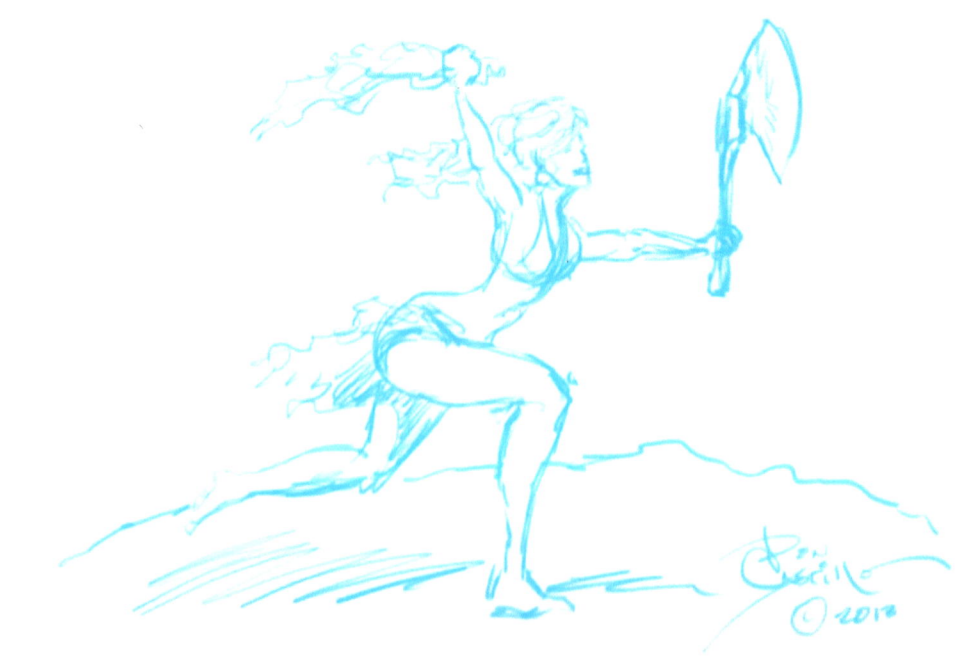

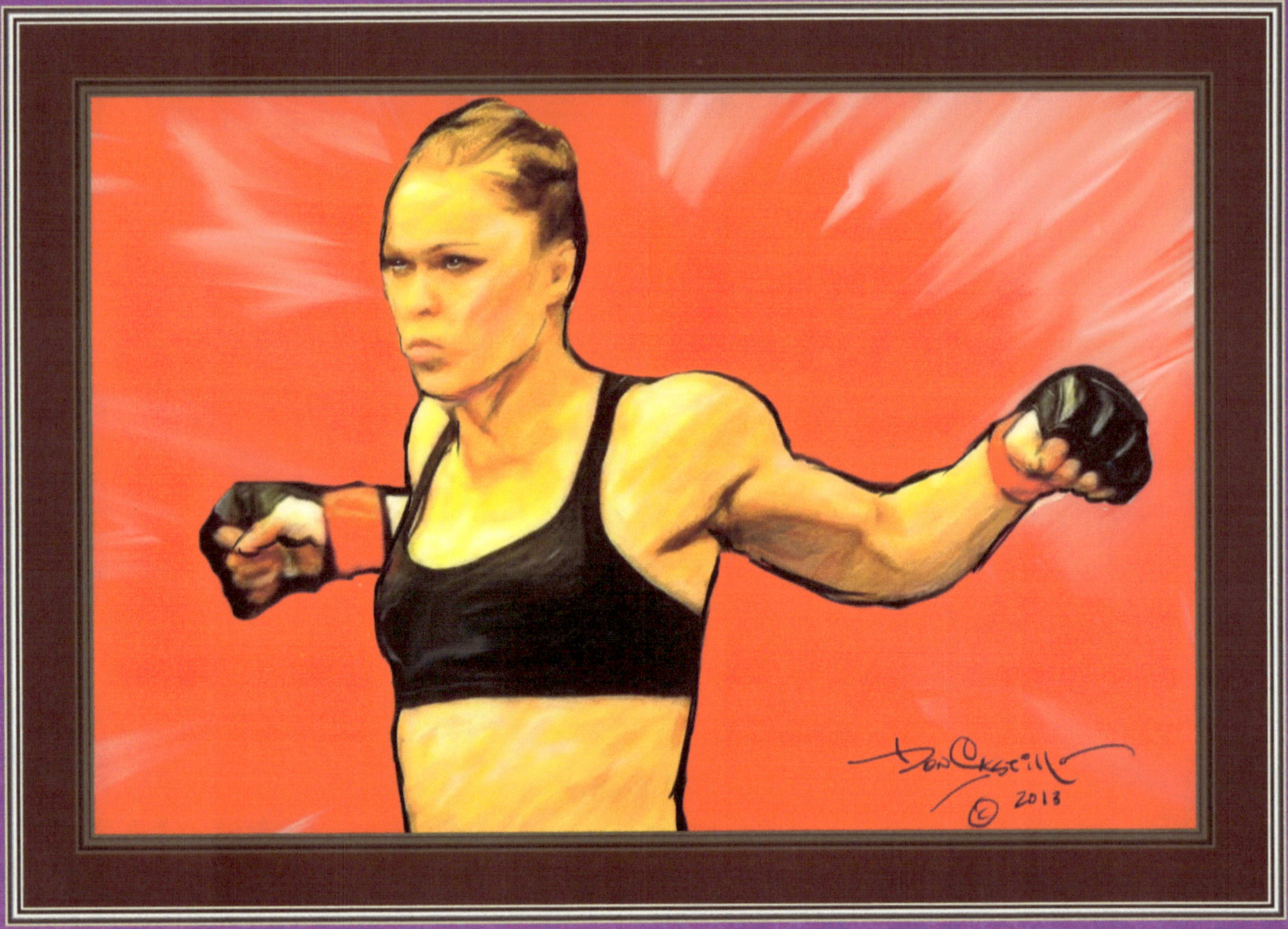

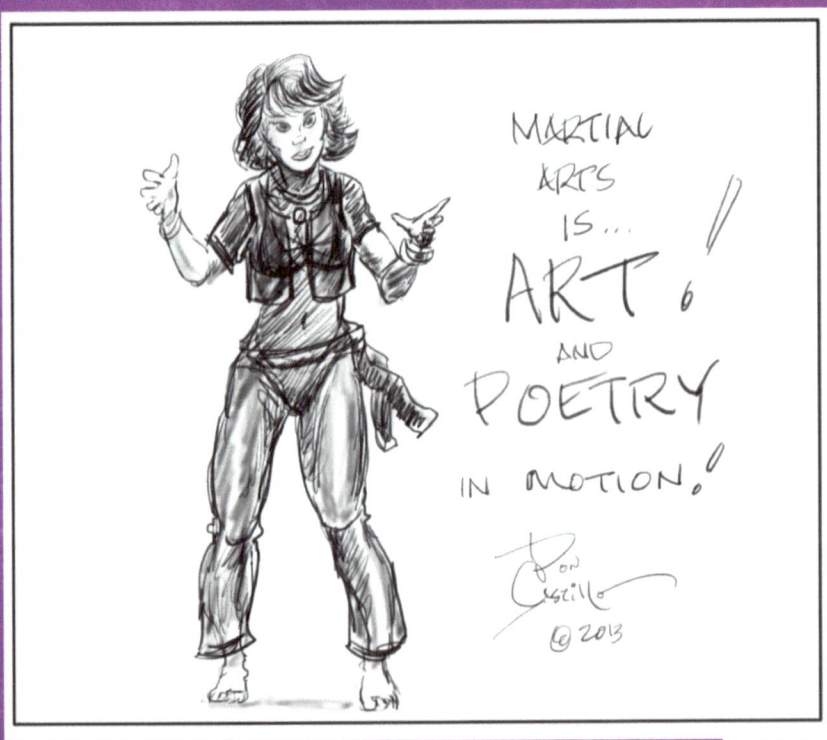

MARTIAL
ARTS
IS...
ART!
AND
POETRY
IN MOTION!

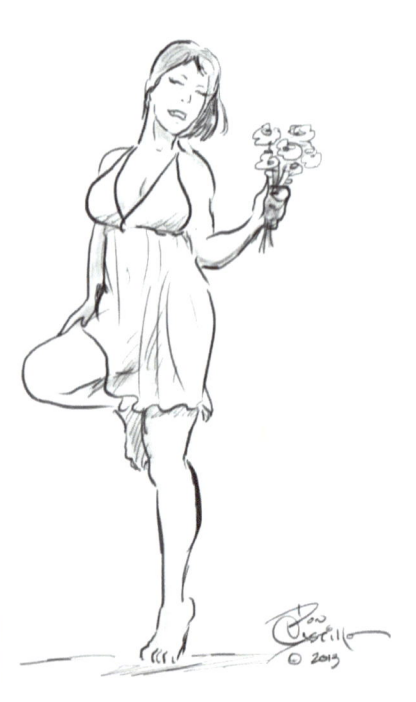

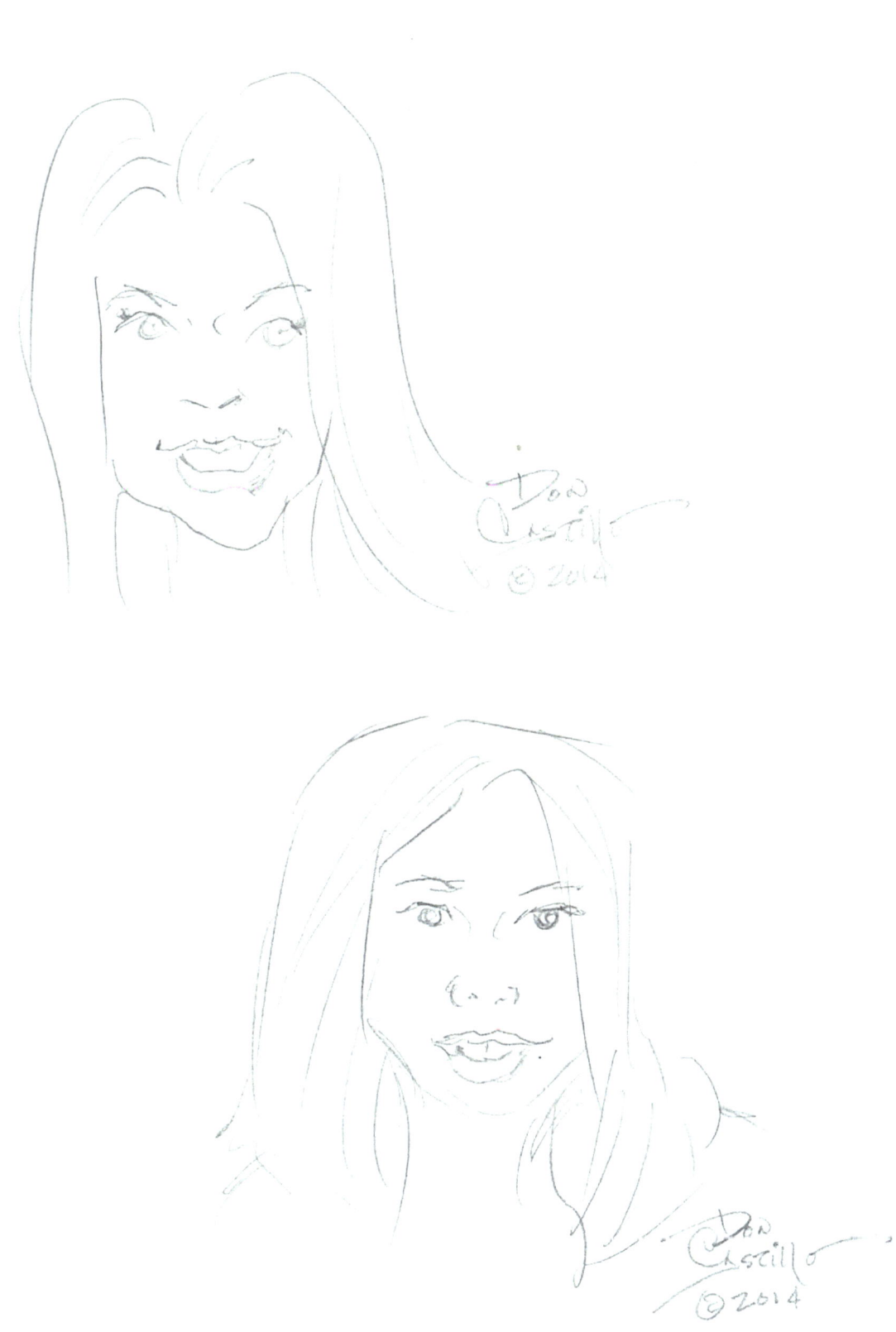

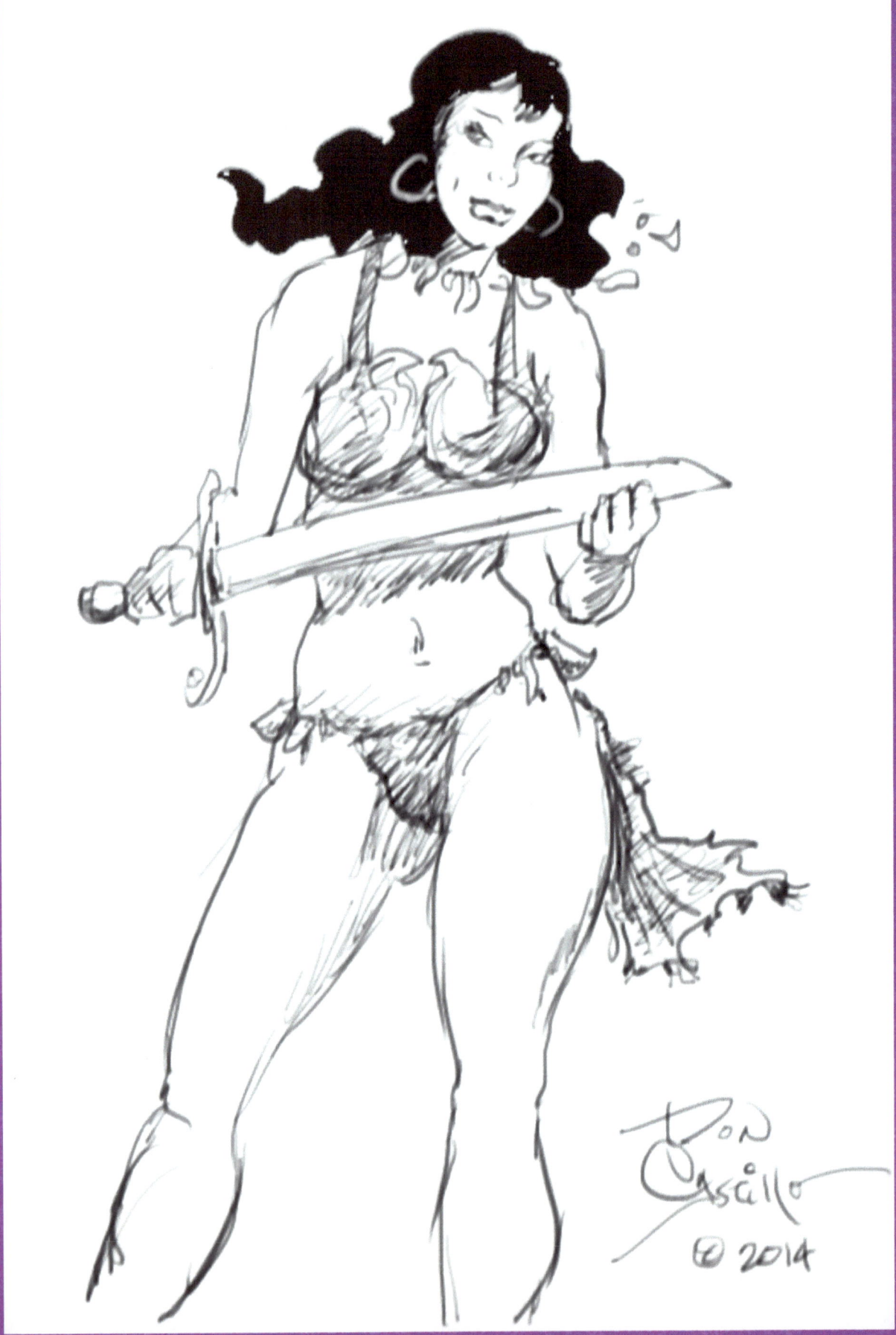

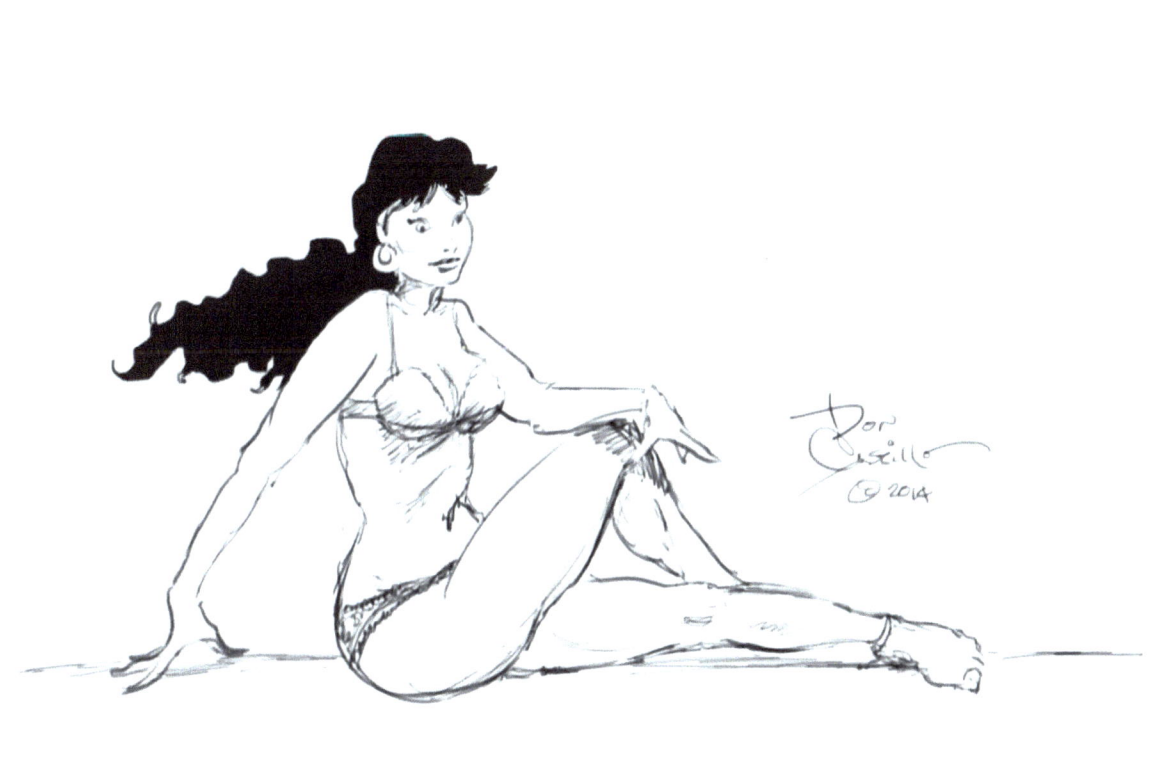

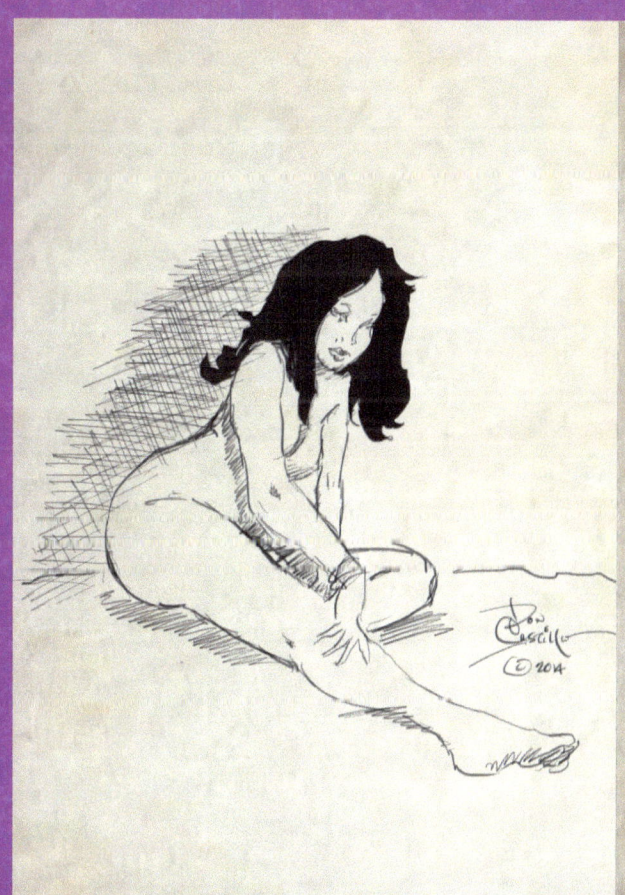

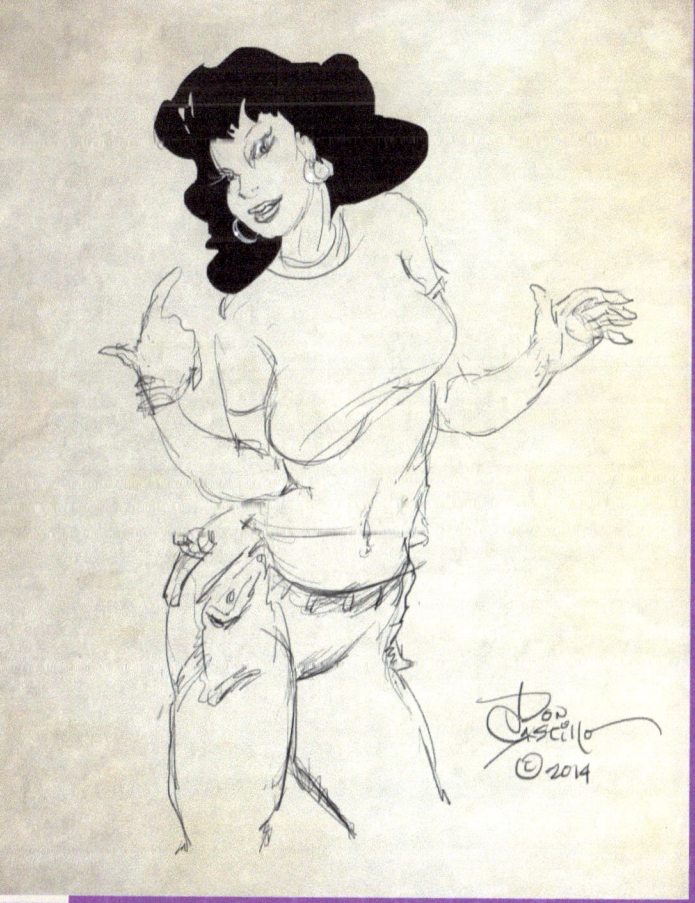

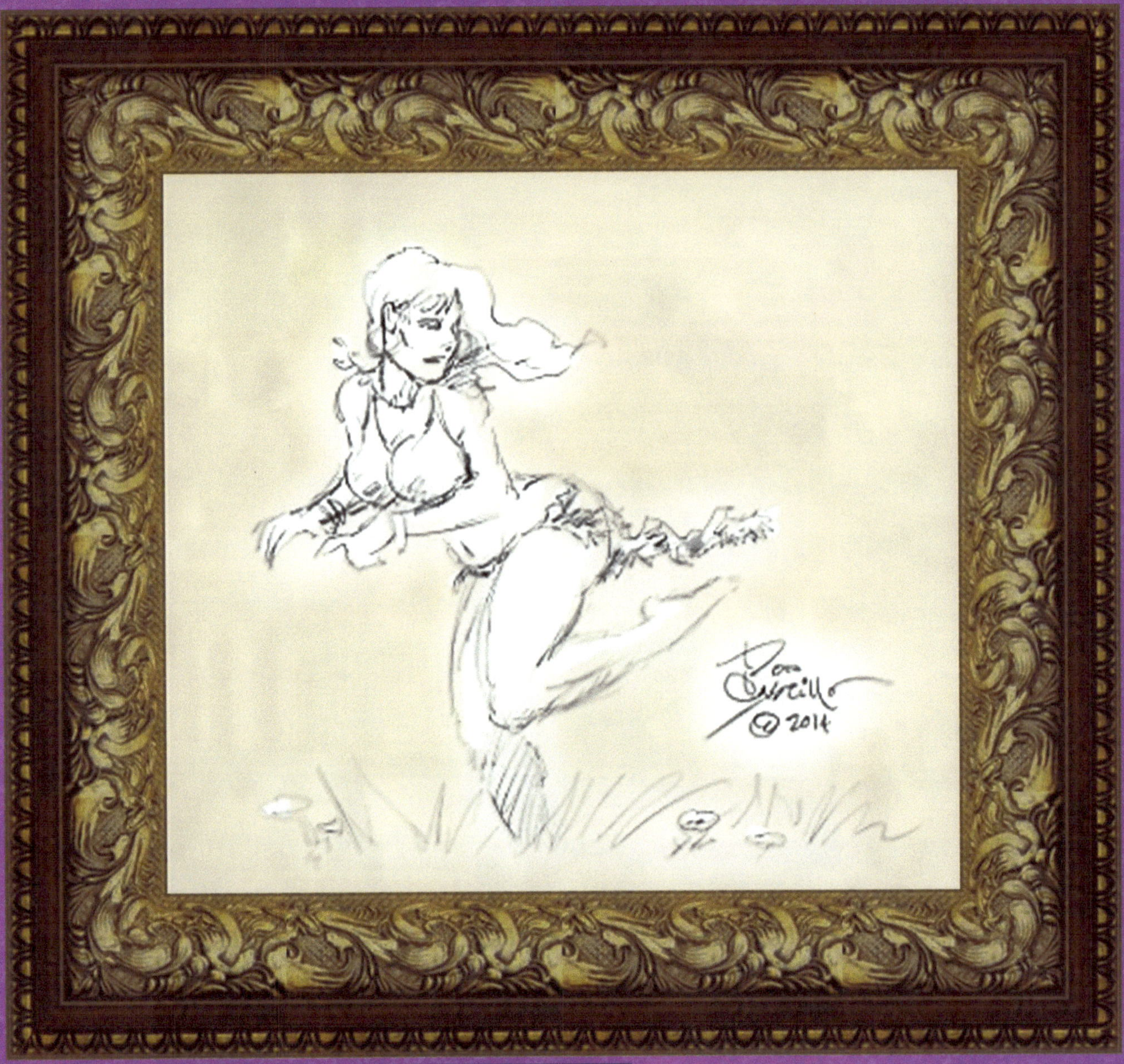

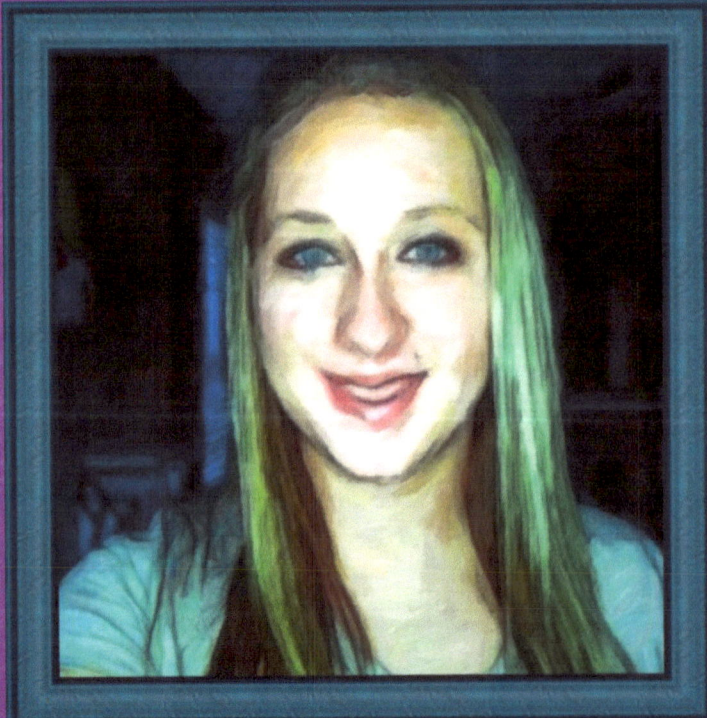
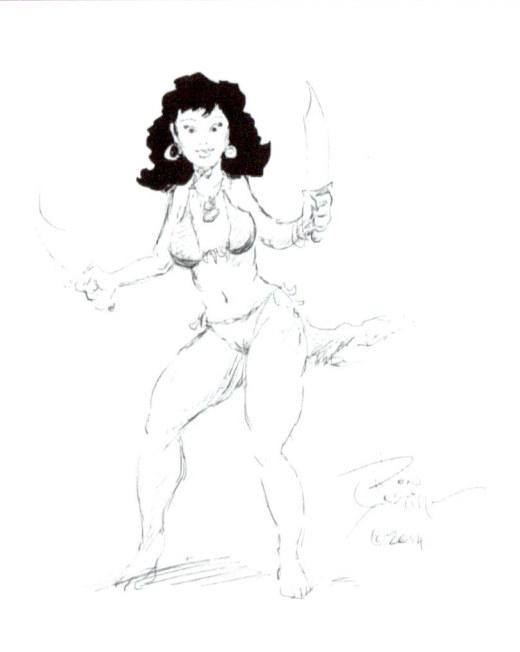

I WOULD LIKE TO DEDICATE
THIS BOOK TO:
MY WIFE TAMMY
AND ALL MY FAMILY
FOR STANDING BY ME
AS I SPENT MANY SLEEPLESS
NIGHTS WORKING ON THIS
BOOK, TO MY DAUGHTER
JILLIANNE LEE CASTILLO
FOR GIVING ME INSPIRATION
TO KEEP GOING, AND TO ALL
MY FRIENDS ON FACEBOOK
AND THE WORLD OVER FOR
SUPPORTING ME,
'THE MARTIAL ARTIST'

THANKS,
DON CASTILLO
LOVE YOU ALL!
FIND ME AT
DON CASTILLO
ON FACEBOOK
OR
DONLEEJKD@AOL.COM

PLEASE LOOK FOR
ALL MY BOOKS
AVAILABLE ON
AMAZON.COM